MW00981422

Healthy Mind, Healthy Body

Healthy Mind, Healthy Body

NEW THOUGHTS ON HEALTH

A
Vedanta Kesari
Presentation

Sri Ramakrishna Math
Chennai 600 004
India

Published by :
The President
Sri Ramakrishna Math
Mylapore, Chennai - 4

VII-4M 6C-11-2004
ISBN 81-7120-800-2

Printed in India at
Sri Ramakrishna Math Printing Press
Mylapore, Chennai - 4

Publisher's Note

When we speak of health, we normally think of only the body. But the health of one's mind is important too. A healthy mind and a healthy body are great assets in the development of a healthy spiritual life. What we need is "total" health. That is the theme of this book *Healthy Mind, Healthy Body*.

All except three essays here first appeared in the December 1997 special edition of the *Vedanta Kesari*. The three new essays are those by Dr. H. Sudarshan, Dr. H. R. Nagendra, and Dr. Ryosuke Uryu. Swami Bhajanananda has revised and enlarged his magazine-article for this book.

The *Vedanta Kesari* edition on holistic health was sold out quickly. Hence this book-version for wider circulation. May all beings all over the world enjoy good health!

Chennai, 16 April 1997
Sri Rama Navami

Contents

Publisher's Note   v

1. Holistic Health
   —Swami Gautamananda   1

2. Health and Spiritual Life
   —Swami Bhajanananda   9

3. Trusting Inner Wisdom
   —Anthony A. Allina   42

4. Native American Healing
   —Pravrajika Vrajaprana   53

5. The Healing Centre
   —Eleanor Foster   67

6. The Need for Holistic Medicine
   —Ralf Damwerth   74

7. Listening to the Body's Inner Voice
   —Carla Martinez   82

8. An Appointment with Life
   —Sam Graci   88

9. Energy Foods for Radiant Health
   —Elvira Graci   96

10. Cancer, Body and Mind
    —Peeyush K. Lala   105

11. Acupuncture
—*M. Lonnie Wu*   121

12. Yoga and Holistic Health
—*H. R. Nagendra*   135

13. Well-being and Spirituality
—*Chris Lovato*   147

14. Tribal Healthcare System
—*H. Sudarshan*   152

15. Holistic Health in Home Care Nursing
—*Nancy Brooks*   162

16. Kai-igaku: The Way of Universal Medicine
—*Ryosuke Uryu*   173

17. Self-Healing
—*Naras Bhat*   184

18. Prisoner of One's Own Habits
—*Anonymous*   198

19. 'Look at the Ocean': A Vedantic View of Health
—*Swami Tyagananda*   202

CONTRIBUTORS   228

1
Holistic Health

SWAMI GAUTAMANANDA

I n the scramble for appropriate technologies, everything including modern healthcare, its goal and practice, is being questioned. The World Health Organization
defines health as 'a state of physical, mental and social
well-being, not merely an absence of diseases or infirmity.'
Really speaking, health is not a state but continuous
adjustment to the changing demands of life and environment. Positive health implies perfect functioning of body
and mind in a given social milieu. Thus holistic healthcare
recognizes the effect of social, economic, environmental and
even political influences on health. Therefore the World
Health Organisation in its drive for 'Health for All by 2000'
proposes to spread health services that are 'relevant, effec-

tive, acceptable and affordable in terms of needs, culture
and resources of each community of the world.'

Till now, strangely, only Allopathic medicine was considered 'scientific' and other indigenous systems, though
based on empirical knowledge, were labelled 'quackery'.
Ideas have changed due to scramble for 'appropriate technologies,' referred to at the outset of this article. Therefore
interest in alternative medicines and medical care system
is growing in the West.

Ayurveda is being studied deeply. Homeopathy is
already being practised even by Allopathic doctors. Psychotherapy, hypnotism, Yoga-therapy, yogic pranayama, and
asanas, etc., are vying for their own place. Everything
seems to be tending towards holistic medicine in accordance
with the concept of 'holistic health.'

For medicine to be holistic, it should be universally
applicable, cover all aspects of health, i.e., physical, mental,
social and spiritual. Some Indian doctors have conceived of
holistic medicine on the basis of the Vedantic *pañcakośa,*
'five sheaths,' i.e., physical body, vital movements, mental
thoughts, intellectual convictions, and emotional feelings
which cover, as it were, each individual soul.

Holistic Health Concept in Vedas

There are several mantras in the Vedas where the
goal of medicine is described as the removal of cause of
death, conferring of long life, purifying thoughts and
actions, removal of the cause of diseases and ensuring the
well-being of body and soul.

Ayurveda, which is called 'a part of the Vedas' (i.e.
Vedanga), is attributed to the sage Bharadwaja (5000 B.C.).

It has a holistic concept of medicare and healthcare and was very popular, being taught even to foreign students in the universities of Taxila, Nalanda and Varanasi during A.D. 500–600. After a decline during medieval period, it is again gaining popularity after the Independance of India in 1947.

Ayurveda defines health as *svāsthya,* 'to be one's own spiritual self.' It is the state of equilibrium of the three principles of air (*vāta*), bile (*pitta*), and phlegm (*kapha*), along with a contented state of senses, mind and soul.

Charaka (A.D. 500–600), the renowned Ayurveda physician, defined health as an equipoised state of body, mind, sense-organs, and soul. This was to him the state of 'ease'. Contrary to this was 'dis-ease'.

Keeping in view the relationship existing between the individual and nature, Ayurveda advocated the following to maintain health and prevent diseases: A daily routine of rising early, exercises, bathing, oil-massage, gargling, and regulated sleep. These must be properly coordinated with the changing seasons. A value-based life was therefore advocated as essential for good health. That an idea of the mental state (*antarātmā*) of the patient is very essential in the diagnosis and treatment of diseases was very much recognized by Ayurveda as follows: 'The doctor who does not find out the inner state of the mind of the patient by the light of his knowledge cannot find out the disease.'

Thus we find that the concept of holistic health is a very old one in India; only it got lost in our daze of the spectacular developments in Western medical science since the last century. Curative medicines have attempted removing diseases from individuals. Specializations and

micro-specializations have made medical care very efficient
but at the same time unaffordable economically to the common man. This last factor is a negative point as far as
holistic medicine concept is concerned.

Maintenance of health through preventive medicines
is another branch which has helped human society to very
nearly get rid of diseases like small-pox, blindness, goitre,
plague, malaria, etc.

Consumerism in Medicare

In the euphoria about the above progress, one should
not forget another dreadful factor that has vitiated the
medical care—the consumerism in medicare prescriptions
of endless investigations and medicines ostensibly to satisfy
the needs of the patient but really to fulfil the greed of
doctors and manufacturers. This has caused great harm to
the patient-doctor relationship. It has caused great suffering to poor patients. Even in advanced countries people
shudder to fall sick. Recently an Indian tourist had to shell
out some fifteen thousand rupees as Medical Insurance cov-
erage of his health for just a two-month period in USA.

Add to this the faulty planning by the Administration
in our country where 80% of health expenditure is made on
20% urban population and 20% of expenditure on 80% of
rural population, and the picture of misery of our poor rural
masses is complete.

Need of the Poor

For medicine to be holistic, we have already said that
it should be universally applicable, cover all aspects of

health, i.e. physical, mental, social, and spiritual. It should also be economically suitable to the common man's purse. Its establishment, buildings and personnel should fit with the common man's cultural milieu. We are sorry to say that the present day urban hospital establishments are frightening and alienating our villagers more than serving them as a shelter in need. Here we may note what some medical men have to say: 'In a developing country like India, the fortunate urban élite have access to almost any highly sophisticated technology either in the capital or abroad while many of the rural poor have no modern medical healthcare whatever.'

Swami Vivekananda & Health

Swami Vivekananda said, 'Serve every person as God.' This concept alone can bring a revolutionary change in our attitudes in medicare. This concept pleads with our doctors and their assistants to consider treatment of their patients as service of God Himself. They would be making their profession itself a spiritual practice, through which great spiritual graces like peace, sympathy, love, freedom and fearlessness can flow.

Swamiji also advocated a regime for healthy food, balanced, nutritious, small quantities taken at several intervals like the Japanese do. He also expressed his opinion clearly on the vegetarian and non-vegetarian food as a health-aid: 'So long as there will be in human society such a thing as the triumph of the strong over the weak, animal food is required, or some other substitute. ... Otherwise the weak will naturally be crushed under the feet of the strong.'

Swamiji also dealt with the genetic causes for the poor physical health of Indians. He said that endogamic marriages within a caste and early marriages were the cause of weak national physique. He further said, 'There is, for example, a good reason for intermarriage in India, in the absence of which the race is becoming physically weaker day by day.'

Priority to the Poor

It is a pity to see our imitation of the West, even in our medical care. We require real courage to resist the materialisitc illusion the Westerners have created. In India our resources are scarce. So we must turn our care more to the poor millions than to the well-to-do, who have other resources to help them.

A sound health education of the masses would be the sure way to improve our national health. The last, but not the least, would be to encourage the spirituality latent in everyone to assert itself, which can work wonders even in medicare.

Latent Powers in the Patient

Even today one can observe in tribal societies that faith in some rites and rituals, chants and talismans with some indigenous herbal medicines, cures many of their ailments. Under extreme stressful conditions, some doctors who believe in spirituality, themselves pray for the patients which gives a psychological resilience to the sufferer.

In the life of Holy Mother Sarada Devi, we find many patients having strong faith getting cured by the use or application of the mud from the temple of Simhavahini in Jayrambati, West Bengal. Many cases of cure of snakebites with the help of this earth have been recorded.

It is now well-known that therapeutic yoga is curing many stress-borne diseases like asthma, high BP, peptic ulcer, nervous diseases, etc., with very little help from herbal and other medicines, but mainly by rousing the vital power through pranayama, the faith power through rhyth-mic chanting of well-known mantras, and through yogasana exercises which strengthen not only the muscles but tone up nerves and the endocrinal glands which help health res-toration marvellously.

Music therapy is another new aid becoming popular as a help to holistic medicare. Prof. Dr. B. N. Manjula, assist-ant professor of psychiatry, NIMHANS, Bangalore, reports that the music therapy reduced to a great extent the mental disorder of the famous mathematical prodigy, Vasisht Narain, at the National Institute of Mental Health and Neuro Sciences. Many other scientists like Dr. E. S. Krishnamurthy, neurologist and psychiatrist, Sri Rama Bharathi, etc. also certify the efficacy of certain musical notes (*rāgās*) of Carnatic music acting powerfully on some mental and neurotic patients to reduce their suffering.

It was Plato who said, 'No attempt should be made to cure the body without treating the soul.' Louis Pasteur, the great French scientist, said, 'Blessed is he who carries within himself God, an ideal beauty, for therein lie springs of great thought and great action.' This brings us to the topic of harnessing spirituality in the scheme of holistic healthcare.

Swami Vivekananda believed that spiritual ideas help cure diseases. He said, 'Even the poison of a snake is powerless if you can firmly deny it.' In another context he said: 'Why are Baburam and Yogen suffering so much? Tell them to meditate for an hour at a stretch, "I am the Atman. How can I be affected by disease," and everything will vanish.'

Conclusion

We thus see that a search for universal systems and practices for human health and cure, from every available source irrespective of its labels like this system or that system of medicine, is in progress.

Here we cannot overlook another major factor contributing greatly to holistic health, i.e., the influence of 'good character' (called also as 'righteous conduct' or 'value-based life'). This rests on the four important values of Truth (which includes honesty, simplicity, etc.), Purity (which includes a controlled sex-life and the sublimation of sexual energies through spiritual channels of philanthropy, selfless service, perfection in all activities, etc.), Faith in one's own divine self (the repository of infinite knowledge, bliss and life), and Fearlessness. A little deliberation will reveal how every one of these values can contribute to the elimination of tensions, stresses, complexes, perversions, and what not, from our private and public life.

Thus we see that along with any education of healthcare and medicare, we have also to impart the importance of the above fundamental values of life. Then alone can holistic healthcare yield results that will last long from generation to generation with ease.

2
Health and Spiritual Life

SWAMI BHAJANANANDA

A common question asked by spiritual seekers is, to what extent they should pay attention to their health. For some seekers this question arises because interest in spiritual life, which is primarily a quest for the eternal, immutable, ever-pure, immortal, infinite Spirit, seems to be incompatible with interest in the ever-changing, impure, limited, perishable physical body. And for those who follow the ideal of social service, concern for their own health appears to be a form of self-centredness. For many other seekers the question of health assumes importance because they soon find that spiritual disciplines, if practised intensely and for a long time at a stretch, can cause several reactions in them (such as arousal of repressed desires, insomnia, etc) which may adversely affect their health.

Two Kinds of Seekers

In this context we may note that spiritual seekers belong to two broad groups, and hence the answer to the question raised above depends upon to which group one belongs.

The first group consists of those who have got intense aspiration which Sri Ramakrishna called *vyākulatā,* restless yearning for God. Intense yearning frees them from all concern for the body and fear of losing health. Endowed with unshakable faith and indomitable will, they keep up unremitting struggle and attain higher spiritual realization, or at least a breakthrough into the transcendental plane, before they pass middle age. Neither mental problems nor physical ailments can deter them from carrying on their struggles.

All the great mystics of the world religions belonged to this group. This is also the tradition that the disciples of Sri Ramakrishna, not to speak of the Master himself, have bequeathed to their followers. But the number of people who belong to this group has always been small.

The majority of spiritual seekers belong to the second group. These people have true aspiration but it is either not intense enough or is not supported by a strong will to undergo prolonged spiritual struggles or to bear the physical and mental reactions that such struggles produce. Many of them do not have any hope of realizing God in this life, and so they are unwilling to sacrifice health or peace of mind for such an elusive and distant goal. It is not possible for them to make spiritual progress their sole concern in life although they may have committed themselves to it in a general way. In their case what is needed is an integral scheme of life in which considerations of health and secular values receive as much attention as spiritual orientation. The present article is meant for this group of seekers.

Body-mind interrelation shows wide variation. There are people who have such a strong physical constitution that their minds have practically no influence on their bodies. Then there are people whose bodies are easily affected by anxiety or strong emotions. Many intellectuals and most spiritual seekers belong to the latter group. These are the people in whom intensification of sādhana results in bodily reactions. It was to help such people that Haṭha Yoga was developed in India. But the exercises of Haṭha Yoga often make the body so sensitive that a slight irregularity is enough to cause serious ailments.

Swami Vivekananda stated: 'How to transcend the senses without disturbing health is what we want to learn.'[1] This is actually a problem which many spiritual seekers face in their lives. Is it possible to intensify sādhana without causing disturbances in the body or body-mind relationship? A positive answer to this question is provided by the holistic health system. Holistic health refers to a wave of health awareness that began in the West in the late 1960s and has now assumed the nature of a movement.

Three Modern Movements

After the Second World War rapid industrialization, urbanization and the breakdown of family life made social life in the West increasingly stressful. The social distur-

bance caused by the Vietnam War, the spread of materialis-
tic ideas and ideals, and the erosion of faith in religion and
morality brought a sense of futility and meaninglessness in
the minds of people. Disillusionment with the promises of
science and technology was followed by the awareness of
the limitations of the Western system of chemotherapy and
the adverse side-effects of antibiotics, sedatives and certain
other drugs. These factors made thousands of people turn to
Eastern philosophies, religious practices and systems of
therapy.

The East, especially India and Japan, responded gen-
erously. And soon, favoured by the social revolution that
swept through several countries in the West in the 1960s,
these countries, especially the USA, came to be flooded with
Gurus, Swamis, Yogis, Roshis, and Lamas. Among the developments that resulted from the interaction of Western
and Eastern cultures, three deserve special mention here.
These are: neo-humanism, interreligious dialogue, and holistic health.

The term 'neo-humanism' refers to a basic change in
modern man's attitude toward himself and his fellowmen
which is characterized by (a) recognition of the essential
goodness of man, (b) focus on existential problems, and
(c) striving for higher spiritual experience. Swami Vivekananda's lectures and work in USA during the last years of
the nineteenth century provided the vital impulse for this
change of man's attitude toward himself. In spite of their
numerical insignificance the Vedanta Societies of the
Ramakrishna movement have made significant contribution
to the development of neo-humanism in the West, although
this fact has not received proper recognition.

The Ramakrishna movement's contribution to interfaith dialogue is in providing an authentic basis for the pluralistic approach to religions. This is widely appreciated. All those who sincerely strive to bring about harmony among the world religions have to recognize Sri Ramakrishna as the originator and the best exemplar of this harmony.

The Ramakrishna movement has not associated itself much with 'holistic health.' This term refers to a modern movement which regards health as a dynamic state of the total human being. It holds that, although the symptoms of a disease may be found in certain tissues or organs, *health* is not mere removal of such symptoms by the treatment of the affected tissues or organs, but a state of multidimensional experience. The mind, body and environment are in a state of dynamic interaction and the maintenance of this interaction in an optimum state of efficiency is what health means. To put it in plain language: 'To be healthy is to have the ability, despite an occasional bout of illness, to live with full use of your faculties and to be vigorous, alert and happy to be alive, even in old age.' This concept of *operational health* has been termed 'wellness'. It is a sense of all-round well-being.

The concept of holistic health originated with small quasi-religious groups of people in the West as a reaction to the analytical-mechanical approach of Western medicine and its inability to respond adequately to the social changes in the 1960s. These groups swelled in number and attracted many qualified medical practitioners. In 1978 the American Holistic Medical Association was founded, and a few years later the British Holistic Medical Association. It is

profitable to know the story of the growth of the holistic
health movement.

Holistic Health

One of the most important aspects of holistic health is
its recognition of the role played by mind in health. This,
however, is not a new idea. Sigmund Freud had shown that
the unconscious played a key role in causing certain diseases which came to be described as psychosomatic
diseases. He looked upon the unconscious chiefly as the
storehouse of negative emotions. His early disciple Carl
Jung expanded the concept of the unconscious to make it
include good emotions and even spiritual urges. Another
follower of Freud, Alfred Adler, showed that the ego could
alter unconscious behaviour. By the early decades of the
present century, psychiatry and clinical psychology had
gained respectability as an authentic part of Western thera-
peutics.

The connecting link between the body and the mind
was still not clear. The supply of this missing link was the
work of the Canadian endocrinologist Hans Selye. In his
classic work *The Stress of Life* Selye showed that mental
stress was the root cause of several types of common illness
such as hypertension, peptic ulcer, etc, although stress itself may have a purely psychological cause such as a mental
conflict or emotional upsurge or the accumulation of 'life's
little hassles.' The original source of stress, known as a
'stressor,' excites the hypothalamus in the brain (through
pathways not yet fully understood). This vital organ which
controls the autonomic nervous system activates the pitui-

tary to secrete the 'stress hormone' (known technically as ACTH) which stimulates the secretion of several hormones and steroids (including the well-known adrenaline or epinephrine). The final result of these changes is the release of more sugar into blood, increase of blood pressure, and various other inner and outer changes in the body, preparing it to face the danger. According to Selye, stress is unavoidable in life and is even necessary for healthy growth. But when it goes beyond a certain tolerance level (which varies from person to person) the system breaks down resulting in illness.

To the scientific picture of mind-body interrelationship given above, certain new concepts were added which did not at first look scientific at all. One was the idea that if negative emotions could cause illness, positive emotions should cause 'wellness'. This idea caught the imagination of the public and the attention of medical experts when Norman Cousins, editor of *Saturday Review,* published a convincing account of his dramatic recovery from a debilitating and incurable disease of the connective tissue. His case also showed the importance of the patient's understanding of the disease and his active participation in the recovery process.

The second idea was that by creating proper awareness within himself man could exercise a certain degree of voluntary control over the healing processes taking place in his body. This is the most difficult and controversial aspect of holistic health. Following Pavlov's demonstration of conditioned reflexes, another Russian scientist K. M. Bykov and his colleagues showed in 1924 that several involuntary processes such as regulation of body heat, blood pressure,

heart rhythm, production of urine, etc, which were medi-
ated by the autonomic nervous system, could be brought
under voluntary control. In later years many experiments
conducted on animals under 'operant' (voluntary) condition-
ing confirmed the above finding. With the development of
the biofeedback technique hundreds of people found that
they could bring under control their heart rhythm, brain
waves, etc. Indian Yogis in the West also demonstrated that
they could alter heartbeat, body temperature etc, simply by
their will power, without the use of any biofeedback instruments.

It was at this point that holistic health practitioners
entered the scene. They showed that not only certain
organs but the working of the whole systems such as the
digestive system, circulatory system, respiratory system,
etc, could be regulated simply by changing one's attitudes
and life-style. It was claimed that even diseases such as
cancer, which were usually regarded as incurable, could be
either cured or held in check by creating the right type of
awareness and strong faith. There might have been a lot of
exaggeration and propaganda in these claims, but the basic
idea that man can consciously regulate involuntary and unseen physiological processes came to be accepted as a fact
by the conservative medical community.

Various contemplation or 'meditation' techniques
derived from Yoga, Vedanta, Zen, and other spiritual traditions were becoming popular in the West in those days. In
traditional religions these techniques have a purely spiritual goal (viz, the attainment of transcendental experience
known variously as Samādhi, Nirvāṇa, etc) and the practice
of these meditation techniques calls for purification of mind

and allegiance to certain metaphysical doctrines. But enterprising teachers showed that 'meditation' also produced other beneficial effects such as reduction of tension, lowering of blood pressure, relaxation of muscles, increase of concentration and work efficiency, and even increase of immunological resistance to diseases. As a result, some form of meditation has become an essential part of most holistic health programmes.

The success of acupuncture and several indigenous drugs, which came to be recognized as 'alternative medicine,' lent much support to the holistic health position. This was further strengthened by two important discoveries. One was the discovery of 'biological clocks' in nature and the existence of biorhythms in the human body. The other discovery was that the brain produced certain neuro-modulators called endorphins which have the property of reducing pain. The production of these natural painkillers is influenced by our thoughts.

Another interesting development in recent years is the application of 'chaos theory' in the field of health. Chaos theory is a mathematical theory applied to nonlinear and random events. It sees order in chaos. Many of the common phenomena in the world such as change of weather, occurrence of heart attack, movement of electrons, the behaviour of cancer cells, etc, do not seem to follow any particular pattern and are unpredictable on the basis of linear mathematics. Chaos theory of mathematics tries to find a more meaningful correlation and behaviour pattern in such systems. One of the most fundamental characteristics of a living being is homeostasis, the maintenance of a fixed internal milieu, especially with regard to body temperature, blood pressure, concentration of salts in plasma, pH, etc. Until recent years, maintenance of homeostasis was regarded as health, and any deviation from it was considered to be disease. But according to current thinking, health is the ability of an organism to respond to an ever-changing environment. Our lungs, heart, liver, etc, are all designed to deal with frequent changes, and health is the capacity to maintain this state of chaos at the optimum level of efficiency.

Lastly, it should be mentioned that holistic health does not reject Western system of medicine in toto. In the case of infectious diseases, nutritional and hormonal deficiencies, and bodily defects which need surgical intervention, it follows the Western system. But in the case of many of the common ailments which have a psychosomatic aetiology such as hypertension, peptic ulcer, allergic asthma, rheumatoid arthritis, irritable bowel syndrome, etc, it holds that these ailments are best dealt with according to the holistic health paradigm outlined above. More important, holistic health provides a way of life which *prevents* the occurrence of some of these ailments.

Integral Life

The Ramakrishna movement has not associated itself with the holistic health movement in any significant way. There are several reasons for this. Though the Ramakrishna movement gives importance to health, it does not make a cult of it. Being a purely spiritual movement with a distinct identity, ideology and global commitments, it has been wary of practices with psychic or occult overtones.

Many of the proponents of the health cult in the 1960s and 70s adopted some of the difficult techniques of Haṭha Yoga. Sri Ramakrishna never encouraged his followers to follow Haṭha Yoga practices. He used to say, 'Hathayogis identify themselves with their bodies. They practise internal washing and similar disciplines, and devote themselves only to the care of the body. Their ideal is to increase longevity. They serve the body day and night. That is not good.'[2] He, however, encouraged the practice of Rāja Yoga. He used to say, 'Rāja Yoga describes how to achieve union with God through the mind—by means of discrimination and bhakti. This Yoga is good.'[3]

It is obvious that the Master's stricture on Haṭha Yoga was directed to its cult of the body which makes people forget God and the supreme goal of life. But the modern holistic health movement has come a long way from its original Hatha Yoga moorings. Holistic health is a neutral force which may be used for material benefit or spiritual benefit as one chooses.

Concern for health becomes an obstacle to spiritual progress only when it is divorced from the spiritual ideal and is treated as an end in itself, or when it becomes an obsession. It, however, becomes an aid to spiritual progress when it is geared to the ideal of God-realization and is properly integrated into spiritual disciplines. As a matter of fact, our main view here is that in integral life, care for health becomes transformed into a spiritual discipline as much as meditation is. What is really needed is an integral vision of life and Reality.

Integral life is not a new concept. It is the ancient Indian ideal of Vedic Ṛṣis. The ancient sages made no

distinction between the sacred and the secular, between the
physical and the spiritual. They realized the unity of life
first—long before they realized the unity of consciousness.
Oneness of life is a fundamental presupposition in every
Upaniṣad. The unitary principle of life was known as
Prāṇa. Cosmic Prāṇa is a major topic of discussion in the
Upaniṣads. The Bṛhadāraṇyaka Upaniṣad describes Prāṇa
as truth (*satyam*), and Brahman as the Truth of truth
(*satyasya satyam*).[4] It may be noted here that it was during
this period (around 500 BC) that India developed the Science
of Life known as Āyurveda.[5]

This integral vision of Vedic and post-Vedic sages was
lost in the later centuries. After the 9th century AD there
set in a progressive decline of interest in the real world, in
anatomy, physiology and medicine, in astronomy and physical sciences. The best brains in India were preoccupied with
the theories of ignorance and illusion, and remained satis-
fied with writing commentaries and glosses on earlier
works. The greatest loss, perhaps, was the loss of the
awareness of the oneness of life and the sacrificial nature of
life. Discovery of the *oneness of consciousness* made all
thinking on the *oneness of life* superfluous. Prāṇa, which
appears in the Upaniṣads as the great cosmic principle of
Life, was reduced to five little winds rattling inside the
belly pushing food hither and thither!

The Tantras which arose between the 6th and 9th
centuries AD evolved an integral view of life far more comprehensive than that of any school of Vedanta. The Tantras
conceive the ultimate Reality as *cit-śakti,* Consciousness-
Power. Matter, mind, and spirit are all regarded as
manifestations of this universal power which is personified

as the Divine Mother. All activities are carried on by the Divine Mother, and all that we have to do is to open ourselves to Her Power through self-surrender and aspiration. But because of their association with certain degenerate practices, the Tantras lost favour with enlightened people, and ceased to be in vogue after the nineteenth century.

For the modern world Sri Ramakrishna has given an integral philosophy of life which combines some of the best elements of the Upaniṣads and the Tantras. Swami Vivekananda revived the Upaniṣadic idea of the oneness of life which he made the basis of his philosophy of service. He also tried to restore the concept of Prāṇa to its original cosmic dimension. But since the front door of philosophical thinking had been closed, the concept of Prāṇa could be introduced only through the 'back door.' And that was how Prāṇa became the chief metaphysical principle in Swamiji's *Rāja Yoga*.

The integral philosophy of life propounded by Sri Ramakrishna and Swami Vivekananda provides a splendid base for the theory and practice of holistic health. In this view physical health is seen as inseparable from mental health and spiritual health.

Conditions of Holistic Health

One point has to be made clear: holistic health is not an easy way to be healthy. It is a difficult path, especially for those who begin it rather late in life. For it entails the sacrifice of some of our ingrained habits, addictions, phobias and obsessions. When pain strikes us in the head or stomach or joints, it is much easier to swallow a pill than

change our eating habits or give up deep-seated hate or
fear.

Holistic health is a programme for activating the
body's own self-renewal processes. It may take months or
years for the body to learn new patterns of response and
renew itself. And the holistic health programme succeeds
only when certain conditions are fulfilled. These conditions
are briefly dealt with below.

Awakening to a New Health Awareness

Most people start on the holistic health programme
only after undergoing an inner conversion. This conversion
may come naturally in the fullness of time or by coming
into contact with a holistic health adept or a yoga teacher.
But more commonly, the inner transformation takes place
only when people have reached the limits of suffering or
when the shadow of lung cancer, heart attack, cirrhosis of
the liver, or some other terminal illness begins to darken
their lives.

Whatever way the change occurs, it takes the form of
two inner processes: a new attitude towards one's body, and
a feeling of responsibility for one's own health.

It is popularly believed that what a person loves most
is his own body. But psychological observation shows that
such an assumption cannot be generalized. Freud himself
at first thought that pleasure seeking was the basic instinct
in man. But years of experience forced him to modify this
view, and he came to the conclusion that, along with life-
instinct (known as Eros), man had an equally powerful
death-instinct (known as Thanatos) which manifested itself

as self-hate and aggressive behaviour. He showed that not all accidents were really accidents. At least some of the accidents were due to the accident-proneness of the victims produced by the unconscious death wish they had cherished. There is enough evidence for milder but insidious forms of self-hate in man. The way many people abuse their own stomachs, lungs and other vital organs, and the way some people bring ruin upon themselves by yielding to drug addiction and alcoholism, indicate how self-hate operates at the level of the unconscious. Most people are unaware of it and drift through life without being aware of the harm they do to themselves. Eventually, however, some of them wake up from this unconscious drifting and begin to have a new attitude—an attitude of love, friendliness and peace towards themselves. It actually indicates the dawn of true love for one's higher Self known as Ātman.

The Brhadāranyaka Upaniṣad in a well-known passage states that everything in the universe—husband, wife, children, everything—is loved for the sake of oneself. What is meant by 'oneself' here? The Gītā speaks of two selves in man—a lower self and a higher Self. The lower self, regarded as a false self, is the sum total of one's instincts, drives and impulses. The higher Self refers to the pure Ātman which is regarded as the real nature of man. The Gītā states that the lower self, if left uncontrolled, will act as one's own enemy and, if purified and controlled, will act as one's own friend.[6] It is the disharmony between the two selves that is the source of self-hate mentioned above. When the lower self is purified and attuned to the higher Self, self-hate disappears and love for the higher Self dawns.

With the dawn of this higher love a person's attitude towards his body changes. He now begins to love his body as an instrument for the manifestation of the higher Self. Hindu scriptures speak of the body as 'the temple of the indwelling Spirit.'[7] As a matter of fact, Hindu temples are modelled after the pattern of the human organism.

Divinization of the body is an important step in Hindu ritualistic worship known as pūjā. Apart from ritualistic worship, service is also regarded as a form of worship known as yajña. Hindu scriptures enjoin five types of service known as *pañca-mahāyajña:* service to gods, service to sages, service to manes, service to human beings, service to animals. And the ancient law-giver Manu says, 'Through the repeated practice of these five great yajñas, the human body gets divinized.'[8]

To look upon the body as divine means to keep it clean, healthy and not to allow any kind of physical or mental indulgence to defile its sanctity and harmony. That is to say, change in attitude towards the body brings with it a new responsibility for one's own health. The surprising fact is that many people think that restoring health and curing diseases are solely the responsibility of the medical profession. In the holistic health system, responsibility for falling ill and getting well both rest primarily with the patient. The doctor only assists him in curing himself.

Knowledge of the Psychophysical Organism

If the patient is to take upon himself the responsibility of regaining and maintaining his health, it is obvious that he should have two kinds of knowledge: knowledge of the specific diseases he is prone to; and knowledge of his own psychophysical constitution.

As regards the first type of knowledge, the recent trend in medical circles is to keep the patient informed about the nature of his ailment and the progress of the treatment. If the patient has a clear understanding of the real cause of the disease, and about his body's inherent capacity to fight the disease, and if he can bear physical pain, at least for a short period, with stoic calmness, he can avoid a lot of unnecessary medication.

In the holistic model, the cause of any disease is understood in terms of the whole person and not in terms of a particular organ or tissue. As the famous turn-of-the-century physician Sir William Osler put it, it is more important to know the patient who has the disease than the disease the patient has. The one person who knows more about the patient than anybody else is the patient himself.

Western science has provided enormous amount of information about the body and also about the mind as independent entities. This knowledge is the result of the painstaking labour of thousands of dedicated scientists for more than two hundred years. This accumulated treasure is humanity's precious heritage, and it would be the height of folly to ignore it or undervalue it. Every educated person should have a basic knowledge of human anatomy and physiology, and also of Western psychology. But it is also important to know that this knowledge provided by science is only analytical and is incomplete.

A more complete, holistic image of man, incorporating the physical, mental and spiritual dimensions of human

personality, was developed in India more than two
thousand five hundred years ago. One of the Upaniṣads
describes the human personality as consisting of five
selves (*ātman*): the *annamaya-ātman* or physical self, the
prāṇamaya-ātman or vital self, the *manomaya-ātman* or
mental self, the *vijñānamaya-ātman* or intellectual self, and
the *ānandamaya-ātman* or blissful self. Many centuries
later, Śaṅkarācārya changed the concept of five selves into
that of five 'sheaths' (*kośa*) covering the pure Ātman. Each
sheath (or self) has its own distinct structure and function
but is in dynamic contact with the other four sheaths. All
the five *kośas* together constitute a single integral personality, each sheath or self representing one level or dimension
of it.

  Furthermore, corresponding to each individual *kośa*
there is a cosmic level of Reality with which it freely com-
municates. The microcosm (*vyaṣṭi*) and the macrocosm
(*samaṣṭi*) are structured on the same pattern and are in
unbroken communion with each other. At the level of the
physical sheath food, water, oxygen, etc, enter the microcosm and carbon dioxide, waste products, etc, return to the
macrocosm. This is true of the other sheaths also: at the
level of each *kośa* something enters the microcosm and
something returns to the macrocosm. The individual cannot
exist independent of the cosmos. If the exchange between
the physical sheath and the physical world around it is
defective, the body will become ill, and when it is stopped
altogether, the body will die.

  A different but parallel model of human personality
was developed by the Tantras. Whereas the Upaniṣads

speak of five *kośas,* the Tantras speak of six *cakras.* In this system, life is regarded as the unfolding of the self at six different levels of consciousness known as *cakras.* In ordinary people the unfolding takes place only at the first three *cakras* which represent procreation, metabolism, and speech; the higher three *cakras* remain dormant. The awakening of the higher *cakras* results in the unfolding and fulfilment of spiritual life.

Another view of human personality is found in the ancient Indian system of medicine known as Āyurveda. This system is based on the Sāṁkhya school of philosophy and conceives life as the interplay of three life principles called *doṣas* or humours (which correspond to the three *guṇas* of the Sāṁkhyas). These are: *vāta* (wind), *pitta* (bile), and *kapha* (phlegm). In a healthy person these three *doṣas* remain in a state of equilibrium. When this balance is lost and one of the humours dominates the bodily system, disease or illness results. Āyurveda also holds that every person has in him a tendency to have one of the three *doṣas* dominate his psychophysical system and, accordingly, human bodies have been classified under three types: Vāta type, Pitta type, and Kapha type. Each shows certain distinct characteristics which are taken into consideration while prescribing diet and medicine.

The models of human personality given above are mutually complementary. They give a holistic and dynamic concept of health. Health is a state of equilibrium of the forces of life within and its harmony with the stream of universal Life outside. Those who want to follow the holistic way of health should try to understand the human personality structure and how life's forces operate within it.

Regulation of Food

Food provides the only source of energy for the human body, and regulation of food intake forms the first practical step in creating health. 'Let your food be your medicine; let your medicine be your food,' said Hippocrates, the father of Greek medicine. In Vedic India when people followed an integral way of life, food was a major topic of discussion even among the sages. Many passages in the Upaniṣads are devoted to a study of the nature and the function of food. The Taittirīya Upaniṣad says, 'Food was verily born before all creatures; therefore it is called the medicine for all.'[9] By stating that food is the panacea (for all ills and illnesses) the Upaniṣad has formulated one of the foundational principles of holistic health. At least half the diseases and ailments of man may be traced directly or indirectly to the problems of food.

Why is food such a big problem? If food were regarded merely as the source of energy and sustenance, it would not have become a big problem in health. But the fact is, food serves several other functions as well. It provides man one of the most elemental forms of pleasure. Most people are addicted to specific types of food, and any change in diet is likely to create deep dissatisfaction in them. Food is an expression of love—love of parents for their children, love of the wife for the husband, love of friends, and so on. Food is also an expression of social and religious solidarity. There is hardly any social or religious function in which sharing of food does not find a place.

Apart from these positive functions, food also serves several negative functions. One negative function which has received considerable attention in recent years is its substitutive role in emotional problems. It has been observed that persons deprived of love resort to eating as a substitute for love. For those who find life empty, eating provides a meaningful activity. Food gives company in loneliness and assuages anxiety and worry. However, the relief felt in these cases is illusory and short-lived. Eating resorted to as a substitute for true fulfilment only aggravates the emotional problem that triggered it. It also usually leads to other problems such as obesity, higher cholesterol level, irritable bowel syndrome, and even abnormalities like bulimia.

By controlling food the whole body comes under control. Control of food means control of both the quality and quantity of food consumed. What really matters is not how much we eat but how much of what we eat is transformed into bioenergy and the building materials of life. Sir William Osler pointed out many years ago, 'Only a small percentage of what we eat nourishes us; the balance goes to waste and loss of energy.'

In holistic health it is important to develop a proper attitude towards food. 'Be thankful for all food,' says Swami Vivekananda in his *Inspired Talks*. 'Food is Brahman.' The Taittirīya Upaniṣad enjoins four vows (*vrata*) or rules on all people:

a) food should not be insulted
   (by not cooking it properly or by wasting it);

b) food should not be rejected;

c) never should a guest be allowed to go without food;

d) food should be produced more.[10]

Summing up our discussion on food, we would like to stress two points:

1. We should develop a proper attitude towards food. Food should be loved for the nourishment it provides, rather than for its taste. Any kind of food which is harmful to one's health should not be eaten. Food should be prepared hygeniçally and should be well cooked. Knowledge of the effects of different types of food on one's system, and a proper understanding of certain specific problems such as lactose-intolerance, allergy to gluten, etc are also a great help in choosing one's food.

2. We should develop a proper attitude towards eating. Eating should be regarded as a sacramental act. In an orthodox Hindu home, food is offered to the family deity first and is then consumed as Prasād. There is a basic similarity between the rituals involved in offering food to the Deity and those involved in eating food oneself. In both the cases, food is offered as oblations to the five Prāṇas regarded as five fires. Even if one does not follow this ritualistic concept, one should make eating a fully conscious and peaceful act. Hurry, worry, anger, distractions, and chattering should be avoided while eating.

Sleep, Exercise, Relaxation

Next to food, sleep and exercise occupy a prominent place in all schemes for health. With the discovery of two types of sleep—REM sleep and non–REM sleep (which correspond respectively to *svapna* or dreaming and *suṣupti* or deep sleep)—a great deal of research has been done on the nature and function of sleep. It is now known that the two types of sleep alternate with each other all through one's sleep at night. Although REM (rapid-eye-movement) sleep is a state of intense brain activity, most people seem to need it for mental and physical health. The requirement of sleep varies from person to person. But six hours of sleep should be sufficient for normal adults. Sleep alters the rhythms of Prāṇa, and often makes the body susceptible to allergic reactions. Holistic health practitioners, therefore, remain careful about their sleeping habits. In the state of dream a person appears to have a different self which often behaves in strange ways quite contrary to the aspirations of the waking-state self. Bringing the two types of self closer to each other and effecting some kind of reconciliation between them is an important task for spiritual seekers.

It is well known that quite a number of modern man's physical problems such as obesity, diabetes, high blood pressure, etc are caused by his sedentary habits. Recent research has shown that moderate exercise helps not only in reducing weight and improving blood circulation but also in controlling degeneration of tissues and neurological disorders like Alzheimer's disease caused by ageing. In a recent article in *Nature,* Carl Coltman has established a clear connection between physical activity and mental ability. Another study has shown that 'even moderate levels of exercise bolster the immune system.' Even the incidence of cancer has been shown to be reduced by regular exercise. Exercise is a good antidote to depression. By working out excess energy, exercise helps in maintaining chastity and in keeping the brain cool. Those who want to spend long hours in meditation should practise brisk walking or some other forms of moderate exercise.

We now turn to another major holistic health concept, namely, relaxation. In normal conditions of life, sleep itself provides sufficient relaxation and there is no need to practise relaxation separately. But under the stressful conditions of modern life, the mind remains in a tense state, and no amount of sleep is sufficient for unwinding it. If you go to sleep with a tense mind, it is quite likely that you will wake up with the mind in the same tense condition.

Stress cannot be avoided in life for the simple reason that nothing great can be achieved in life by leading a stress-free, easy-going life. We have to work hard, face the problems of life, shoulder responsibilities, encounter evils of different kinds, live with incompatible people; and all this causes stress. Even spiritual life, which involves inner struggles, can cause a good deal of stress. What then should we do? We should try to reduce stress as much as possible and should learn to deal with the type of stress which cannot be avoided.

Countermeasures against stress include certain spiritual techniques such as prayer, meditation, cultivation of the witness attitude, and practice of self-surrender to God which enable us to avoid a lot of unnecessary stress. Along with these, special relaxation exercises, preferably yogic exercises, must be practised. Several excellent books on these exercises written by enterprising yoga teachers are available now and so this topic is not dealt with in detail here.

But three points need to be noted in this connection:

1. Relaxation does not mean simply lying down, doing nothing. Relaxation very often necessitates some physical movement or exercise in order to stretch the muscles which are in a tense condition. Some of the *āsanas* or postures

become more effective when converted into dynamic exercises.

2. Everyone has a specific region in his body which acts as focal point for his mental tension. For some it may be the heart region, for others it may be the pit of the stomach or lumbar region. Choose that type of yogic exercise which will relax the muscles and tendons of the specific focal point of tension in you.

3. There is perhaps nothing more relaxing than the practice of regulated breath. It is not necessary to practise Prāṇāyāma which can lead to serious complications. What is needed is the practice of *breathing in* deeply (as deeply as possible) through both the nostrils and then slowly *breathing out* (without retaining breath). This kind of regulated breathing can be done at any time, even in your office while talking to people.

These simple relaxation exercises can alleviate psychosomatic pain felt in the head or stomach or joints more effectively than pills and tablets.

Finally, everyone should know his stress-tolerance level, that is, the amount of stress he can bear without breaking down. By leading an austere life and by doing vigorous exercises he should try to raise his stress-tolerance level.

Attunement to Biorhythms

Along with regulation of food, sleep, exercise and relaxation, the spiritual aspirant should learn to attune his psychophysical system to his own biorhythms.

The understanding of biorhythms began with the discovery of 'biological clocks' in animals in the late 1950s. For instance, mussels and crabs which live on seashores were found to open their shells or become active according to the rise of the moon (which caused the flow of tide) even when they were removed to a distant place. Then followed the discovery of 'circadian rhythms' in the human body. It was found that body temperature, blood pressure, level of sugar in the blood, production of hormones and enzymes, etc, changed according to a cyclic pattern. Most people have 24 or 25 hour cycles; some have 36 or 48 hour cycles. It has also been found that, apart from physiological activities, even emotional sensitivity and intellectual creativity increase and decrease according to biorhythms.

There are daily biorhythms, lunar rhythms, and annual rhythms. Some people (the 'larks') are early risers and are alert and active in the morning, whereas there are others (the 'owls') who feel dull in the morning and hit the peak of efficiency at night. Similarly, there are 'lunar' and 'solar' people. In the case of lunar people the 11th day of the lunar month (the *ekādaśi,* regarded as fasting day by orthodox Hindus) or the day of the full moon or the day of the new moon may act as the pivotal point of change in their biorhythms. Some people have 28-day cycles irrespective of the movement of the moon. The solar people (often described as Apollonians) are more sensitive to changes of season than to changes of the moon. They may find profound changes taking place in their physiological processes and mental activity with the onset of winter, spring and other seasons.

People with gross minds may not be able to detect these biorhythms, but hundreds of studies have not only confirmed the existence of these rhythms but have also shown their astonishing regularity. A spiritual seeker should recognize his biorhythms and adjust his prayer, meditation and activities in accordance with these rhythms. He should not feel perturbed by minor stomach upsets, pain in joints, disturbed sleep, change of mood, etc, which are associated with biorhythms.

Removing Mental Blocks

One of the reasons why holistic health practices often fail or succeed only partially is that Prāṇa or life energy does not flow freely within the individual or between the individual and the universal life, owing to the presence of obstructions within. These obstructions are caused by *saṁskāras,* residual traces of our past actions and experiences. Saṁskāras are of two kinds: those which produce only memories (*smṛti*) of past experiences and those which produce impulses or drives to repeat those experiences. The latter are called *vāsanās.* Vāsanā and smṛti are interlinked to form complex patterns of love, hate, fear, and other emotions. It is these 'complexes' that obstruct the free flow of life energy in us.

Many of these complexes are formed in childhood and adolescence. When unpleasant or traumatic experiences take place, the tendency of a child or teenager is to repress them. Repression is a process of pushing the saṁskāras of past experiences into the unconscious regions of the mind. The growing youth may not be able to recollect those bad experiences again, but the repressed saṁskāras lodged in the hidden recesses of the unconscious go on creating psychological and psychosomatic problems for him.

Unless these repressed complexes are ferreted out and confronted, holistic health techniques alone will not cure psychosomatic disorders completely. The seeker has to dive deep into his unconscious, encounter the past experiences, and deactivate the past saṁskāras. Owing to repression, this is a difficult process. Most people find it difficult to do it without the active help of a competent guide. Those who depend on God through intense prayer may, however, find that these inner blocks are removed through divine grace. This is how faith healing and miraculous cures take place.

Extension of Consciousness

Life is a great healing power. Life not only creates, sustains and destroys, but also heals. At the physical level the healing power of life manifests itself as (a) self-renewal and (b) the immune system.

The capacity of the body to filter and re-use its fluids and repair damages to tissues, especially skin and bone, by growing new cells has been known for many years. But modern research has shown that self-renewal is constantly taking place in every part of the body. With the exception of certain brain cells almost all the cells in the body, including those which constitute the hard bones, are constantly being replaced by new ones. It is said that almost the entire body gets renewed in this way every year. This shows that it is never too late to regain your health. Even in old age it is possible to overcome the damage to the body caused by years of misuse and neglect and gain a fresh lease of life by changing one's basic attitudes and way of living.

The human immune system is one of the great marvels of this universe. Anyone who knows about it and

also about the biochemical processes going on in the body
will find no exaggeration in Walt Whitman's famous words,
'To me every hour of the day and night is an unspeakably
perfect miracle.'

Our immune system consists of four units: the
granulocyte-macrophage unit, the lymphocyte unit (consisting of B-cells and T-cells), the antibody unit, and the
complement unit. The first two are varieties of white blood
corpuscles, whereas the last two are chemicals, proteins. As
soon as a few bacteria break into any tissue in the body, the
four units of our immune system launch a concerted attack
on the invaders. Who masterminds this attack? Who plans
the strategy? Who coordinates the logistics and deployment
of our internal defence? Somewhere behind all this there
must be a master control. But why does it sometimes go
awry, as it does in autoimmune diseases like rheumatoid
arthritis, when our defence units mistake our body cells for
enemy microbes and attack the innocent cells? Why do certain normal cells become malignant and start attacking
neighbouring cells? Western medical science is trying hard
to find answers to these questions.

In the integral view developed in ancient India, life is
not regarded as restricted to certain activities going on in
cells. Rather, life is a universal stream of consciousness-
power known as Prāṇa in the Upaniṣads and *Cit-śakti* in
the Tantras. Each living being represents a centre around
which Prāṇa moves at different levels known as *kośas* or
sheaths. At the core of this multistoreyed personality structure is the locus of the Ātman, the true self of man, in the
form of a powerful light. The Upaniṣads state that just as
the spokes of a wheel are fixed at the hub (*arā iva*

rathanābhau), so also Prāṇa and all psycho-physical structures are fixed at the Ātman. The Ātman is the master
controller of life that Western science has been seeking. The
'sheath of intelligence' (*vijñānamaya-kośa*), also known as
the buddhi, dhī, and heart, is where the light of the Ātman
is experienced.

The Ātman, though unattached, exercises its power
through the will (known as *dhṛti*), which in Indian psychology is regarded as the dynamic aspect of buddhi. With the
help of the pure will (*sāttvika dhṛti*) a yogi is able to keep
all his sense organs, all activities and mind under control,
says the Gītā.[11] Acquisition of this pure will is the result of
a spiritual awakening. This awakening, which takes place
only through prolonged and intense spiritual struggles,
opens the mystic door in the heart. This gives the yogi access to all the *kośas* or sheaths of the personality structure.
He gains the capacity to open each *kośa* to the stream of
cosmic Prāṇa. The stream of universal life flushes out
impurities and diseases from the personality system and
brings in new vigour and strength.

This kind of higher yogic self-mastery is, of course,
possible only for a few people who strive intensely for it.
But everyone can maintain an inner alertness and some
degree of general supervision over all his activities such as
eating, sleep, exercise, response to stressful situations, etc.
It is the failure of this inner watchfulness, known as
prajñāparādha or 'Fault of Awareness,' caused by ignorance
and negligence that makes a person yield to evil thoughts
and deeds, to diseases and ailments. *Caraka-saṁhitā,* one
of the most authoritative books on Āyurveda, states: 'What
is known as "Fault of Awareness" produced by the distor-

tion of intellect, will and memory, is the cause of the disturbance of the three humours.'[12] In other words, carelessness,
lack of alertness, forgetfulness, misuse of will power—this
is one of the main causes of disease. *Prajñāparādha,* 'fault of
awareness,' is a very significant phrase. The root cause of
most of the psychosomatic or constitutional disorders is
prajñāparādha, the misuse of our cognitive and conative faculties. It is our unconscious way of living that is the
primary cause of illness.

Naturally, the way to restoring health is to cultivate
conscious, self-directed way of living. Hyperacidity, rheumatoid arthritis, irritable bowel syndrome, and similar
disorders are the body's ways of drawing our attention to
the needs of certain organs. Simply by extending our consciousness into the interior parts of our body we bring these
unknown and neglected areas closer to the light of the Self
and bring about integration of personality. This integration
stimulates our immune system and restores the coordination, rhythm and balance in the working of the different
organs. This kind of extension of consciousness can be done
in various ways.

One of the most well-known of these methods is
biofeedback. Various other techniques have been developed
in modern times such as autogenic training, Vipassana,
eurythmics (coordination of sound and body postures, developed by Rudolf Steiner) etc. The most effective way of
extending awareness, however, is through meditation.
Absorption in meditation leads to inner awareness which
can then be extended into the affected part of the body
through concentrative visualization. When this kind of extension of meditative awareness is practised for some days,

the processes of self-renewal and self-defence get acceler-
ated and healing takes place. Even if this does not take
place, meditation brings about relaxation in a natural way.

Opening the System to Divine Sakti or Cosmic Prana

Those who find it difficult to follow these techniques
can open themselves to the source of divine Power through
intense prayer. In the Gītā the Lord promises that He takes
care of the spiritual and material welfare of those who
depend on Him alone through constant remembrance.[13] By
cultivating an attitude of trust, self-surrender, and receptivity we can also open ourselves to cosmic Prāṇa. When
such a prayerful attitude becomes deeply ingrained in our
psyche we find everything in Nature becoming favourable to
us and the process of healing begins in our psychophysical
system. Thousands of people all over the world have found
health, prosperity, and peace through prayer. Prayer over-
comes the resistance of the ego and opens the chambers of
the unconscious to the inflow of Divine Śakti or Cosmic
Prāṇa. For this, however, prayer must be done with intensity, sincerity and perseverance. Only through this kind of
prayer can we know how prāṇic healing takes place.

Let us now recap the basic principles of holistic
health: Awakening to a new health awareness

> Knowledge of the psychophysical organism
> Regulation of food, sleep, exercise
> Relaxation
> Attunement to biorhythms
> Removing mental blocks
> Overcoming *prajñāparādha*
> Opening the system to Cosmic Prāṇa.

These principles may appear to be difficult at first, but as the ancient Greek writer Plutarch has stated, 'Choose the best life, and custom will render it agreeable.'

REFERENCES

1. *The Complete Works of Swami Vivekananda,* 8 vols. (Calcutta: Advaita Ashrama, 1978), 6: 129.

2. *The Gospel of Sri Ramakrishna,* trans. Swami Nikhilananda (Madras: Sri Ramakrishna Math, 1980), 579.

3. Ibid., 331.

4. *Bṛhadāraṇyaka Upaniṣad,* 2.3.6.

5. Originally there were two main schools of Āyurveda: (a) the Ātreya school founded by Agniveśa (around 700 BC) whose work was revised by Caraka in AD 100 under the name Caraka-saṁhitā; (b) the Dhanvantari school founded by Suśruta (around 600 BC) whose work is not traceable. What is now known as Suśruta-saṁhitā is Nāgārjuna's redaction of the earlier work done around AD 200. In the 8th century a new system known as Siddha system was added.

6. *Gītā,* 6.5–6.

7. देहो देवालय: प्रोक्त: स जीव: केवल: शिव: । —*Maitreyī Upaniṣad,* 2.1

8. महायज्ञैश्च यज्ञैश्च ब्राह्मीयं क्रियते तनु: । —*Manu-saṁhitā,* 2.28

9. अन्नं हि भूतानां ज्येष्ठम् । तस्मात् सर्वौषधमुच्यते । —*Taittirīya Upaniṣad,* 2.2.1

10. *Taittirīya Upaniṣad,* 3.7–10.

11. *Gītā,* 18.33.

12. धी-धृति-स्मृतिविभ्रष्ट: कर्म यत् कुरुतेऽशुभम् ।
प्रज्ञापराधं तं विद्यात् सर्वदोषप्रकोपणम् ॥ —*Caraka-saṁhitā,* 1.102.

13. योगक्षेमं वहाम्यहम् । —*Gītā,* 9.22

3

Trusting Inner Wisdom

ANTHONY A. ALLINA

My mother and I barely survived my birth. Modern medicine kept us alive, and did so again several times during my lifetime. I watched with amazement as man walked on the moon and, later, I would participate in these miraculous events by assisting my surgical colleagues open up and repair human hearts. It seemed all the secrets of life were being discovered by science, and I definitely wanted to know those secrets. I studied science, then medicine in school and eagerly became a physician. I couldn't bear being left out of this most impressive arena of life. The University of California Medical School at San Francisco provided a high speed, high pressure, inside look at the workings of science and medicine, and trained me well in the ways of modern medicine.

Medical school encouraged me to become the coldly rational, all knowing, scientific doctor, which was entirely consistent with society's vision of a doctor, or for that matter of a businessman, lawyer or other professional. Knowledge was everything, and within its towering shadow, we got the job done. But something was missing. I came to realize that the larger my fund of medical knowledge grew, the weaker the connection to my inner life became. Eventually, through the sheer bulk of medical work, the pursuit of knowledge displaced most other activities. The brilliant light of scientific mastery blinded teacher and student alike to an invisible, modern American epidemic that continues to the present. It might be called a deficiency disease or 'soul loss.' As doctors, there was no time for the soul, or inner spirit; we were all too busy, and I was one of the victims. In fact, there was a standing joke among medical students that for each year in medical school, we would need two to recover. We underestimated.

Consequently, for the doctor, soul loss was the unsuspected by-product of an over-emphasis on scientific knowledge, and, as might be expected, for the doctor's patient the same overemphasis had occurred. This was indeed a pervasive imbalance of modern Western civilization, manifested as the irrelevance of our inner life and overvaluation of our functional role, our outer productivity. The possibility that this imbalance might be the source of illness wasn't even considered by mainstream medicine. But times have changed. More recent investigations have indicated that inner disconnectedness is a significant factor in producing disease. For example, medical research has discovered that the most powerful predictor of first heart attacks in men under the age of fifty is not high cholesterol, nor high blood pressure, nor smoking, but job dissatisfaction. When men do not feel a meaningful connection to their work, it can kill them. I see this as a manifestation of soul loss: a 'soulless' connection to work. It is very stressful to live without a meaningful connection to our lives and our activities, and it is well established that stress is a significant cause of disease.

To address this very personal and culturally pervasive problem, I ventured into meditation, and later, Jungian analysis. In my attempt to assist patients to find the most productive path toward good health, I began to integrate the medicine of the body with that of the mind and spirit. To ignore any one of them would be incomplete.

By the time I opened a private general practice office in 1978 I had learned Autogenic Training, a meditative technique described by Carl Jung as 'Western Zen.' My psychologist partner and I had taught this technique to individual patients and groups at the University with overwhelmingly positive results. This technique, abbreviated AT, was tremendously helpful for me in coping with the stresses in my own life. I felt more centred, less disjointed. I enjoyed teaching AT to patients to help treat various illnesses, and found that they too felt less frantic and more grounded. AT was a valuable tool to add to my medical bag. It joined my stethoscope and scalpel.

I taught AT to Rick, a fifty-year-old businessman with chronic back pain and high blood pressure. He was a big, handsome looking, former football player, and an intensely competitive, extremely successful man. He was always active in his approach to life's problems; he was also quite anxious most of the time, and described shaking or trembling when the time came to go to work. He worked hard because that was what he was trained to do; and he made a lot of money because that was what was expected of him. These were his two most important orientations in life. I taught him Autogenic Training because he objected to taking all the medications needed to control his illnesses. It was very difficult for him to understand how AT, a passive, receptive technique, could possibly be useful; it was not his style. Over many months, Rick and I met for hour-long appointments. I taught him AT and I listened as he talked about his life, his expectations and his disappointments. As he learned how to meditate, his medical problems decreased, and not unexpectedly, he began to find some relief from his constant angst. For him, the experience became so pleasurable that he would leave work sometimes twice a day just to meditate. He said that it was the ONLY time he really felt good. He enjoyed a feeling of peace, of being centred, no longer feeling as dissociated or frazzled as he had most of his life.

It gives me great pleasure to see patients discover the inner peace that AT provides. With that serenity, new doors open and many are able to get beyond previously insurmountable obstacles; they get unstuck, they get healthy. However, it is not a quick fix. It takes time and personal, intimate interactions with patients, for which rapid fire, mechanistic medicine does not make space. The time spent can be richly rewarding, especially when the diseases are proclaimed incurable by scientific medicine. The grounded, centred state of consciousness afforded by meditation can be therapeutic when medication and surgery cannot. In fact, in ancient medicine, illness was considered a result of an improper relationship with 'the Gods,' or inner self in modern vernacular. Healing occurred when the proper alignment to the inner self, or 'the Gods,' was reestablished. When experiencing the peacefulness of meditation, it does indeed feel like a proper realignment of consciousness with some eternal 'inner' self, some fundamental element of our unconscious. The process of finding that deep, inner voice requires a receptive and attentive state of consciousness. Westerners often value a more aggressive approach. Control and domination reign supreme in our masculine oriented world. Western society places very little importance on receptivity. When we enter the more feminine, receptive, mysterious state of consciousness, we experience the balancing of the masculine, rational mode. We become a more complete being. When the yin and yang are in balance, then we are whole. Meditation allows the inner self to be heard. The voice within is beautifully different for each person. I have learned that the discoveries are richly rewarding. Lila's story illustrates the importance of honouring the process of finding one's own meaning to treat illness.

Lila developed a serious, life threatening, auto immune disease. Usually our immune system attacks outside invaders and protects us from bacteria or viruses. Instead, Lila's immune system generated an attack on the cells of her own body. It is as though the immune system failed to differentiate properly between 'self' and invader. It 'sees' the self as a dangerous invader and attacks.

Lila's disease progressed from mild to severe within months. A specialist told her that the disease would kill her. In fact, modern medicine had no cure to offer her. Yet somehow she knew that she would not die from this disease; her inner voice had said so. She put all her energy and determination into discovering the meaning of her illness. We studied it together. We explored any promising treatments. I became her consultant in a treatment process which she determined. I encouraged some of her choices even when they were in violation of scientific medicine, and in the process she taught me a great deal about disease and the threat of death as a powerful motivator. She tried medication, acupuncture, herbs, bee stings, a special diet, and other therapeutic modalities. I remained supportive of her various attempts at treatment, and helped evaluate their effect. Eventually she came to trust in, and be guided by, her inner spirit which clearly brought dramatic changes in her life-style and appreciation of life. She began to get well. The disease had been stopped. For the past seven years she has discovered that when she remains close to her innermost spiritual path, her disease remains quiescent. When she meanders back into the frantic, disconnected distractions of soulless American 'busy-ness,' her illness flares. She now feels grateful for her disease because it has directed her to a meaningful and, for her, a deeply spiritual path. She feels intimately and personally connected to all the activities in her life; for Lila everything is sacred. She radiates the kind of spiritual aliveness of one who follows her own inner path. Her disease led her to it; her disease keeps her on it. Lila's story is remarkable and for me the lessons are extremely important. The journey was Lila's, not mine. I didn't cure her. I only supported her while she sought her own unique path. I reinforced the value of listening to her innermost being. She did it beautifully and courageously.

How does this healing process work? Human beings are always engaged in the process of healing. We are constantly healing the daily wounds of a normal existence. This three-million-year-old human body would not still exist were it not for this inborn ability. Current concepts of cancer, for example, include the notion that we are repeatedly growing cancerous cells, and just as quickly killing them. Again, it is our immune system's ability to identify the invader and then to attack and eradicate it that protects us. When this system fails we become ill. It is also well known that this system can be markedly affected by a variety of factors, including emotional events, such as grief or anger. There is a link between our physical bodies and our inner selves. Maintaining a healthy inner life is as much a necessity for a healthy body as diet and exercise. Restoring a healthy, balanced inner life can be as important or even more important in treating illness as is surgery or medication, though all these approaches have their place. How can we influence this balance? Meditation is one method; Lila's intense inner-directed work with her illness is another. A third method is visual imagery.

Susan makes this dramatically clear. She had been treated for a painful sinus infection in one sinus for six months by the best specialists, but to no avail. Despite multiple medications and a dozen codeine pain pills per day, she remained ill. The next step in her treatment would be to drill a hole in her forehead and drain the infection to prevent it from spreading to her brain. She refused to accept surgery as her only option. She already knew how to meditate and agreed to try visual imagery as well. She had nothing to lose. As she meditated, I asked her to allow the pain in her head to paint a picture in her imagination. The image that came to her was of a garage from her childhood full of green slime. This image was so disgusting that it actually made her vomit every time she 'saw' it. Eventually we were able to suppress the vomiting, which allowed her to continue with the process. She quickly realized that the slime needed to be removed from the garage, but without dumping it into the surrounding environment. She solved the problem by sending out a septic tank truck and some workmen who drilled a hole in the garage and inserted the hose from the truck. They sucked out three truckloads of slime, disposing of it safely. At that moment, she had no pain. That day the X-ray was normal for the first time in six months. The disease was gone; this was eighteen years ago. Susan had made use of her own inner resources to cure a disease that seemed resistant to all forms of medical treatment. The explanation for exactly how this occurred is not found in Western medicine, but I think the key is being able to form a communication link between the body and the innermost psyche, or unconscious. I like to view this as an exploration of, or 'fishing' in, the unconscious. Somehow this permits the normal physical processes that keep us healthy to operate unhindered; it helps us overcome obstacles to good health.

In the same way that the scenes in the imagination are portrayals of physical problems, I believe that physical illness can be a metaphor for, or reflection of, the contents of the unconscious. Is it possible that the running wild of a single cell line in leukemia or cancer is the physical manifestation of a similar overly dominant intrapsychic process? Or that the over reactivity to harmless pollens in allergies is reflective of a similar state of hypervigilance in the psyche? These types of provocative and fruitful questions permeate my medical work. Here is another case that makes this psychosomatic connection clear, and describes yet another method of 'fishing' in the unconscious, dream analysis.

Dr. Robert Grinnell, an internationally renowned Jungian Analyst and my own analyst, described this case to me. He had seen a 28-year-old man with severe, uncontrollable grand mal epilepsy. The patient's electroencephalogram (brain wave test) indicated a right frontal lobe abnormality, or scar, which was the focal point for and cause of his seizures. Neurologists had prescribed a variety of anti-epileptic medications but were unable to completely control the seizure activity. One night the patient had a dream in which there was a catamaran like, bi-hulled oil tanker: an explosive image. In the right front hull the crew was planning a mutiny against the captain. Dr. Grinnell pointed out that the dream seemed to paint a picture of the epilepsy with a right frontal lobe origin. The dreamer was asked what the nature of the crew's complaint against the captain entailed. Once this was recalled, the patient never had another seizure and the electroencephalogram became normal. He was cured of his epilepsy. However, he was plunged into a prolonged depression while trying to resolve the vexing issues brought to consciousness by the dream. Once it was brought to consciousness, his body was no longer obliged to act out this inner conflict. To me, as a physician, this is an extraordinarily impressive therapeutic technique: another tool added to my medical bag.

In Jungian analysis one works toward a more complete knowledge of one's own wholeness, a process called individuation. Psychological growth can be arrested in many ways. Getting stuck can disrupt the healthful balance that our bodies know how to maintain which makes us more susceptible to disease. When disease does occur, dream analysis is one method that can assist patients in finding a way of getting past the obstacles that are impeding their growth and thereby restore their bodies to health.

The case histories I have described underscore the central role of the patient in the healing process. Patients are not the passive recipients of treatment, but are vital participants in the pursuit of restoring and maintaining their health. This type of healing requires that the belief system of the patient be amenable to such an approach. When a patient is not comfortable with this approach I respect their convictions. I pull out my stethoscope and write a prescription.

Trusting the inner wisdom of the individual lies at the heart of the medicine that I practise. I encourage my patients to get in touch with their inner knowledge. Healing involves a relationship, superficially between doctor and patient, but more importantly between the self and the soul. With the time constraints imposed by the current fast-paced, mechanistic medical system, I often feel frustrated in my attempts to balance an impersonal scientific approach with a more humanistic one. It distresses me deeply to conform to the requirements of medical insurance and reduce my patients to numbered illnesses with numbered treatments. I have been referred to as a dinosaur: the kind of practitioner that will not survive in this era of assembly-line medicine, but that remains to be seen. For me, however, there really isn't much choice. I know that we human beings have great inner resources that are often crucial to our health and well being, and I will continue to nurture those seeking that path. Meditation alone can be therapeutic by quieting the often disruptive voices of the conscious mind, and allowing a more peaceful, less frantic energy to direct the body. Therefore, I will continue to teach it to those who want to learn. I also know that deep personal meaning can be found in illness, and so I will continue to encourage my patients to search for their own meaning and employ visual imagery and dream analysis in that process. I will also provide them with all the wonderful options that modern medicine has to offer.

In my practice I try to create a bridge between the objective scientific domain and the subjective personal realm. To me, medicine is not one or the other, it is both. I am grateful for the opportunity to practise medicine in this way and to interact with my patients on the intimate level that this approach requires.

4

Native American Healing

PRAVRAJIKA VRAJAPRANA

A word, please, before we begin. It is difficult to discuss the broad topic of Native American healing simply because there are hundreds of Native American tribes whose spiritual traditions and healing practices vary widely from tribe to tribe. Some healing ways are specific to the tribe; others are specific to the medicine person who heals. But while tribal and individual differences cannot be disregarded, there are some general principles of healing that all Native American tribes share. We can try to understand and appreciate these wider principles as we approach them from some specific Native American perspectives.

When you hear the word 'medicine,' what image comes to your mind? A spoonful of vile-tasting liquid, choked down with closed eyes and pinched nostrils? Or perhaps your image of medicine is more sanitized: a tiny white pill, discreetly ingested three times a day.

For traditional Native Americans, the standard Western concept of treating illness is healing gone topsy-turvy. In contrast to Western pills and potions, 'medicine' for the Native American means spiritual power and divine mystery. The Lakota word for healing medicine, *wapiya,* literally means going back to the right order. And like *dharma,* the right order is spiritual.

The Native Americans' most basic premise regarding health is that healing cannot be separated from spiritual life, and spiritual life and physical health cannot be separated from one's daily life. Native American spirituality allows no pigeonholing. Further, one's individual existence cannot be separated from the rest of the community, nor can the individual and the community be separated from the rest of the cosmos. A Cree medicine woman, Rose Augur, remarked, 'Modern medicine cannot heal the things we can. . . . We don't just focus on the physical being, we focus on the whole human being, that's the mind, physical, spiritual, and emotional. Every part of a human being must be addressed in order to heal. And it does not stop there, it involves the whole family, and then the family involves the community.'[1]

For the Native American, the term 'holistic health' is oddly redundant: 'health' in itself means being connected in a meaningful way to the community and the cosmos; 'health' means having the physical, intellectual, emotional and spiritual aspects of one's personality integrated into a seamless whole. This integrated vision of life is the very

definition of wellness since the one inviolable truth of existence is that *everything* is connected to everything else.
When this truth is compromised, the inevitable result is
imbalance, illness; it is manifested physically, mentally,
and spiritually in the individual; an out of balance individual throws the community off-balance, and this process
reverberates in the world at large. 'To tribal people,' Carol
Locust wrote,

> healing cannot be separated from worship or from daily life.
> Worship is not contained in a building or limited to certain days,
> but is on-going every minute of life. Personal health is a con-
> tinual process of keeping oneself strong spiritually, mentally,
> and physically, and in doing so, keeping away or overcoming
> those forces that might make one unwell. To remain well,
> individuals must stay in harmony with themselves, their
> environment, and their Creator. Harmony thus becomes a shield
> against disharmony. . . . Added to the harmony may be herbs,
> rebalancing of energy, and rituals of fasting, prayer, and thanks-
> giving to the Creator.[2]

In the Native American worldview, a human being is
composed of three inseparable components: body, mind, and
spirit. Illnesses are 'directly related to a spiritual cause,
creating an imbalance between the body, mind, and spirit.
Cause and effect, action and consequences, have strong
implications in healing.'[3] The law of cause and effect—what
we generally call 'karma'—has long been recognized as a
crucial element in Native American healing traditions. All
actions have their consequences; any transgression of individual and community moral codes (which are simply the
laws of the universe writ small) is a moving away from the
'right order,' and this bears a direct consequence on an individual's health. At the heart of every Native American

healing ritual is the attempt to put back into balance what
has gone awry. 'Every case of sickness and pain has its
reason,' the Shoshone medicine man Rolling Thunder said,

> and it's always a price that's being paid, either for something
> past or something future. But that doesn't mean we're not sup-
> posed to do something about sickness and pain. The important
> thing is to know how these things work. Modern doctors—most
> of them—don't seem to understand that. A medicine man's job
> is to look into these things. We know that everything is the
> result of something and the cause of something else, and it goes
> on like a chain. You can't just make the whole chain go away.
> Sometimes a certain sickness or pain is meant to be because it's
> the best possible price for something; you make that go away
> and the price becomes greater. The person himself may not
> know that, but his spirit knows it. That's why sometimes we
> [medicine men] take up to three days to look into things before
> we take a case, and we may not take it at all.[4]

If Rolling Thunder can speak so confidently about
what a medicine man's job is, our next question might be,
What *is* a medicine man or woman? Answering this question involves unravelling a larger cosmology.

Every Native American spiritual tradition affirms the
reality of a divinity that rules the cosmos and whose sacred
presence pervades every aspect of and every activity in the
world. The power of this divinity pervades all things, but
some things are more sacred than others—for the Lakota,
the buffalo are sacred animals; for the Navajo, corn is a
sacred plant.

Some human beings also possess more spiritual power
than others. This person may simply have been born with
more spiritual power than others, or, more likely, the power
may have come from a visionary experience. A powerfully

important spiritual tradition among the Sioux and other Plains tribes was the *hanbleceya*—the 'vision quest,' also called 'crying for a dream.'

Generally first performed in youth, the 'lamenter' fasts and prays alone in the wilderness for four days. During this time of intense austerity (the lamenter has neither food nor water and has only a blanket for protection against the extreme elements), the spiritual seeker directs his or her entire mind to receiving spiritual wisdom through a vision or dream. Lame Deer, the Minneconjou Sioux medicine man, recalled his first vision quest:

Suddenly I felt an overwhelming presence. . . . Then I heard a human voice, strange and high-pitched, which could not come from an ordinary being. All at once I was up there with the birds. I could look down, even on the stars, and the moon was close to my left side. The voice spoke: 'You are sacrificing yourself here to become a medicine man. In time you will be one. We are the fowl nation, the winged ones, the eagles. You shall be our brother. You are going to understand us whenever you come up here to seek a vision.' . . . Then I saw a shape before me. . . . I saw that this was my great-grandfather, Tah'ca Ushte, Lame Deer, Old Man chief of the Minneconjou. I understood that he wished me to take his name. This made me glad beyond words. Again I wept. This time with happiness. I don't know how long I had been up there, one minute or a life-time. I felt a hand on my shoulder gently shaking me. It was Uncle Chest who had come for me. 'You have been up here for four days. . . . Time to come down.' I was to tell him everything that had happened to me and he would interpret my vision so that I could understand what they meant. He told me also that I was no longer a boy, that I was a man now. I was Lame Deer.[5]

Visionary dreams also can lead an individual to become a healer. Brave Buffalo was 73 when he was

interviewed in 1918. He became a medicine man as a result
of a dream he had when he was a boy:

> When I was ten years of age I looked at the land and the rivers,
> the sky above, and the animals around me, and could not fail to
> realize that they were made by some great power. I was so
> anxious to understand this power that I questioned the trees and
> the bushes. It seemed as though the flowers were staring at me,
> and I wanted to ask them, 'Who made you?' I looked at the
> moss-covered stones; some of them seemed to have the features
> of a man, but they could not answer me. Then I had a dream,
> and in my dream, one of these small round stones appeared to
> me and told me that the maker of all was *Wakan Tanka* [the
> Lakota word for the Creator, the Great Mystery], and that in
> order to honor him I must honor his works in nature. The stone
> said that by my search I had shown myself worthy of supernatu-
> ral help. It said that if I were curing a sick person I might ask its
> assistance, and that all the forces of nature would help me work
> a cure.[6]

The Yaqui tribe presents another view of Native
American medicine and medicine people. *Seataka* is the
Yaqui word for the innate mysterious power that all beings
possess. Although this power pervades everything, it occurs
in greater concentration in spiritually gifted people.
Seataka is the power that cures illness; to be a healer, one
must possess this power to a greater degree in order to
transmit its power to others. In an individual, *seataka*

> expresses itself in a love and concern for all other people,
> animals, plants, indeed, all of nature. The person possessing
> *seataka* is friendly and helpful to other people and is well liked
> in return. He volunteers to help in time of trouble and illness.
> He likes to play with children and tell them stories. He is kind to
> animals, giving them food and water and never harming them.
> He is fond of flowers and other plants, tends them in a garden,

never breaks off their blossoms, leaves, or twigs wantonly. He has a keen appreciation for the beauties of nature. He dreams vividly during his sleep, and his dreams are meaningful in foretelling the future. . . . He is clairvoyant, able to see things happening at a distance. . . . He learns things 'naturally'; 'he just knows' without having to study.[7]

Not surprisingly, Native Americans have always deeply honoured their medicine men and women. Like the brahmins in India, respect was accorded medicine people because they led noble, exemplary lives and had dedicated themselves to spiritual practices and service to humanity. Fools Crow of the Teton Sioux nation said:

> I do not argue, do not fight, do not hate, do not gossip, and I have never said a swear word. I have not chased after women, and I have controlled my lust for them. I have not charged for my curing, healing or advice, although I have accepted the gifts of gratitude people have brought to me. I have never touched alcohol or drugs. . . . One of the reasons why I have had such a hard time trying to find people to pass my medicine on to is that there are so few who want to live morally and frugally.[8]

The purpose of leading a pure life was to become, as Fool's Crow described it, 'a hollow bone.' A true medicine man or woman is merely the instrument of *Wakan Tanka,* the Great Mystery. A hollow bone has no will of its own; it is content to be used, to let the power of God flow throught it without the slightest impediment. 'The cleanest bones serve *Wakan Tanka* . . . the best,' Fools Crow said, 'and medicine and holy people work the hardest to become clean. The cleaner the bone, the more water you can pour through it, and the faster it will run. . . . The holy person is the one who becomes the cleanest of all.'[9]

How does one become 'a hollow bone'? According to
Fools Crow, 'You must love everyone, put others first, be
moral, keep your life in order . . . and have a good character.'[10] When that happens, what is the result? The healing
power of *Wakan Tanka* is passed through the medicine person to the individual who needs healing. 'The power comes
to us first to make us what we should be, and then flows
through us out to others,' Fools Crow explained.[11]

Again, like brahmins in India, Native American medicine people were the repositories of a tribe's spiritual
wisdom, mythology, and history; for this reason, they were
the true bedrock of Native American culture. Perversely,
the pivotal role accorded them *because* of their innate goodness made their eradication one of the foremost objectives
of their conquerors. Their very existence was deemed the
greatest barrier to the 'civilizing' process imposed upon Native Americans. John Bourke said that only 'after we have
thoroughly routed medicine men from their entrenchments
and made them an object of ridicule' could whites 'hope to
bend and train the mind of our Indian wards in the direction of civilization.'[12]

That this so-called 'civilization' could not succeed in
this endeavour is undoubtedly one of the greatest triumphs
of the human spirit. Ironically, the same civilization that
tried to annihilate Native American culture is now, a century later, humbly seeking to learn its ancient wisdom. A
small but significant number of university-trained health
professionals are now beginning to seek the wisdom of Native American healers. Healing, they now realize, involves
more than what can be written on a prescription pad.

Rolling Thunder observed that 'healing requires knowing more than the body.' Continuing in this vein he added, 'If a modern M.D. sees a sick man, he sees the sickness and not the man. If the doctor doesn't understand . . . what the problem really is, if he then gives someone chemicals so the man won't feel anything or if he finds some troubled part of the body and cuts it off and throws it in the trash, it's probably all unnecessary, and it certainly isn't healing.'[13]

For the Native American, the healing process involves not only every aspect of the individual, but the community that enfolds him or her as well. As one Dr. Ackerknecht despairingly noted in his article on 'Primitive Religion': 'The participation of the [Native American] community in the healing rites, and the strong connection between these rites and the whole religion and tradition of the tribe, produce certain psychotherapeutic advantages for the medicine man which the modern physician lacks.'[14]

For Native Americans, a healing ceremony is a community affair. In the Navajo tradition, healing is done with sand painting. There are approximately 500 different sand painting designs and for each sand painting there is a specific healing chant (many of which are famed for their haunting melody) to accompany it. The medicine man diagnoses the source of the illness; relatives and friends are also actively involved in the healing process. Not only do they observe the sand painting process and participate in the long hours of chanting and prayers, a family member or friend may easily ride on horseback 50 miles to obtain but one of the many herbs to be used in the ceremony. For the healing ceremony even to take place, the individual's family and friends must actively support and participate in the whole healing process.

Assembled on the floor of a house, the sand painting recreates the entire Navajo cosmos, including those mythic characters who have some connection to the cause of the illness. The sand painting is carefully constructed according to the medicine man's memory since no visual record is kept of sand paintings. Cornmeal—considered sacred by the Navajo—is sprinkled on the sand painting and on the patient who then walks onto the painting and sits in the middle of it. Attuned to the symbols and power inherent in the sand painting, the patient and the painting, the individual and the cosmos, become united. The sand painting ceremony, which includes many hours of chanting and prayers led by the medicine man, brings the patient back into harmony with the cosmos. Disharmony was the real cause behind the illness; harmony has now been restored.

The sand painting 'represents . . . the spiritual and physical landscape in which the patient and his or her illness exist, the etiology of the disease, and the mythological narrative that has been chosen for its cure. . . . The chanting and vigil bring disperse elements together. . . . The patient suddenly sees her sickness and her life together, joined in the cosmos, everyone she knows and cares about singing and praying for her. There is a reason for her to want to get well, and there is all the support she could imagine.'[15]

The cosmos, the community and the individual have been restored to wholeness. The final chant joyfully rings in the blessings of the newly healed individual:

> Happily I recover
> Happily my interior becomes cool
> Happily my eyes regain their power
> Happily my head becomes cool
> Happily my legs regain their power
> Happily I hear again
> Happily for me the spell is taken off!
> Happily may I walk in beauty![16]

The patient healed, the sand painting is destroyed.

Native plants and herbs of all varieties have always been used by Native Americans for healing purposes. Noble Red Man, an old Lakota, cured his diabetes through the use of bitter wild berries. The American physicians who diagnosed his illness were astonished to find that his debilitating illness was suddenly nonexistent. When questioned by the doctors, Noble Red Man remained silent. Later he said, 'God gave us medicine to share with people, but if the white man gets his hands on it, he'll charge you a great price and will let you die if you don't have the money. God's medicine is free. God doesn't charge a fee. We don't give money to God. We give Him our prayers, our thanks. And sometimes we give Him the only thing that's really ours . . . our pain.'[17]

That's all very nice, we might say, but what does this have to do with me and my life? None of us are going to track down a sand painting in Arizona or build a sweat lodge in the backyard. Nor are we going to traipse through the woods in search of sacred herbs. What can Native American healing practices offer non-Natives to make this more than a pretty anthropological picture, bereft of practical application?

'Not everyone can be cured,' the Sioux medicine man Fools Crow said, 'but everyone can be healed.' Most physicians would find such a statement incomprehensible, but for Native Americans, curing relates only to the physical body, while healing relates to the whole human being. 'Healing is purely spiritual,' Fools Crow continued, 'and has to do with helping a person to be right with *Wakan Tanka.*'[10]

From the Native Americans we can learn that the basis of all health is spiritual. Whether we call it Brahman, God, or *Wakan Tanka,* the basic truth of our existence is centred in that Reality. When we move away from that truth, we suffer physically, mentally, and of course, spiritually. The basis of wellness is a God-centred life.

Native American healing philosophy also teaches us that the individual is inextricably nestled in the community; individual wellness is linked to the physical, mental and spiritual health of the community. The Zen monk Thich Nhat Hanh has said that happiness is not an individual matter. Native Americans have shared this belief for thousands of years: community well-being is created by individual well-being and vice versa. The Native Americans remind us that we are all connected to one another. As human beings we cannot afford to reject portions of the community as not being an integral part of ourselves. As we watch societies implode while their inner cities slide into chaos, we would do well to remember this point. The Lakota medicine man Mad Bear said:

You [white] people have such anger and fear and contempt for your so-called criminals that your crime rate goes up and up. Your society has a high crime rate because it is in a perfect position to receive crime. You should be working *with* these people, not in opposition to them. . . . It's a mistake to think of any group or person as an opponent, because when you do, that's what the group or person will become. It's more useful to think of every other person as another *you*—to think of every individual as a representative of the universe.

Every person is plugged into the whole works. Nobody is outside it or affects it any less than anyone else. Every person is a model of life . . . I don't care how low you fall or how high you climb . . . you still represent the whole thing. Even the worst criminal in life imprisonment sitting in his cell—the center of him is the same seed, the seed of the whole creation.[19]

From the Native American healing tradition we can learn that we serve best when *we*—that is, we as ego-bound individuals—get out of the way. The more our hearts become purified, the more the ego diminishes and the more the power of the divine can move through us without impediment.

Finally, we can learn from the Native Americans prayerfulness, patience, and forgiveness. Were it not for these qualities, the Native American healing traditions would have been destroyed long ago; it would not be the resurgent spiritual force that it is today. Rolling Thunder said, 'The medicine power is not dying out. In fact, it is coming again to many of our young people. Years ago they were saying that one day there would be no medicine people; but we were not fooled at all, we knew that we would not die out. We knew that one day, as though it had begun overnight, the power would be seen to be returning again. Now it is coming back strong.'[20]

REFERENCES

1. Sandy Johnson, ed., *The Book of Elders: The Life Stories and Wisdom of Great American Indians* (New York: Harper Collins, 1994), 145.
2. 'Traditional Medicine,' Mary B. Davis, ed., *Native America in the Twentieth Century* (New York: Garland Pub., 1994), 642.
3. Ibid.
4. Doug Boyd, *Rolling Thunder* (New York: Dell Pub. Co., 1974), 123.
5. Richard Erdoes, *Crying for a Dream* (Santa Fe, NM: Bear & Co., 1989), 28.
6. Peggy Beck, Anna Lee, Nia Francisco, eds., *The Sacred: Ways of Knowledge, Sources of Life* (Tsaile, AZ: Navajo Community College Press, 1977), 22.
7. Mary Elizabeth Shutler, *Ethnic Medicine in the Southwest,* ed. Edward H. Spicer (Tucson, AZ: University of Arizona Press, 1977), 187.
8. Thomas E. Mails, *Fools Crow: Wisdom and Power* (Tulsa, OK: Council Oak Books, 1991), 40.
9. Ibid., 36.
10. Ibid., 42.
11. Ibid., 31.
12. Virgil Vogel, *American Indian Medicine* (Tulsa, OK: University of Oklahoma Pr., 1970), 35. Quoting 'The Medicine-Men of the Apache,' *Ninth Annual Report, Bureau of American Ethnology, 1887–88,* 451; 594.
13. Boyd., pp. 123–24.
14. Vogel, p. 34.
15. Richard Grossinger, *Planet Medicine* (Berkeley, CA: North Atlantic Books, 1995), 213; 215.
16. Erdoes, p. 111.
17. Harvey Arden, ed. *Noble Red Man: Lakota Wisdom Keeper Mathew King* (Hillsboro, OR: Beyond Words Pub., 1994), 56.
18. Mails, p. 136.
19. Boyd, pp. 244–45.
20. Ibid., 263.

5
The Healing Centre

ELEANOR FOSTER

A fresh breeze comes through my open window. I breathe it in and feel its health move through my body. I breathe more deeply and it fills my lungs, lightens my limbs. My spirit turns for a moment to thankfulness, knowing itself a part of the universe.

I am a psychotherapist. I meet with people who are troubled, whose minds and emotions leave them no rest. I sit with them and hear their pain as clearly and freshly as I can, sometimes it enters my own body. Then I must breathe deeply and find my own stillness. I want to help them, but I know that I am not the healer. I do not believe that in the end their healing will come from anyone outside themselves. I can only turn them towards their own healing.

I believe that healing comes from within. It is my deep
faith, both as a therapist and as a Quaker, that within each
of us is a source of life and health, a divine centre, 'that of
god.' Through tangled remembrances, bitter fears, self-
confusion, this stillness can emerge. We can learn to turn to
that source, and return to it again and again. We breathe it
in, the freshness engages us. We are more whole.

It is also my conviction that if we turn to this centre
deeply enough and stay with it truly enough, we will find an
even wider healing. We will find compassion growing, a
gentle awareness that others share our same struggles, our
imperfections, our yearnings. We will begin to understand
that we are all one. The divine centre is love.

But the fullness of health cannot be hurried. Scabbing
over a wound too quickly without the slow steady growth of
new healthy tissue only leads to festering and breakdown.

A woman comes to me wanting support to leave an
alcoholic husband, but perhaps already wishing for another
to carry the burden of her expectations and dependencies.
How can I encourage her to move into her own strength, to
reclaim the sense of her inherent worthiness? Her body
listlessness, her sallow skin, lead me to think she herself
may have missed out on the early loving which brings happiness to a child's gait and bounce to their flesh, a
well-being that lingers into adulthood. It may be that for a
while, perhaps for quite a long while, she will need to have
her store of self-respect replenished by my steady loving
regard for her, and by my confidence in her being able to
find her own way. She will also be encouraged if she is able
to meet with others who are determinedly taking their own
steps towards selfhood.

The way to self-dependence is slow and difficult, full of traps of bitterness and loathing and self-pity. If this woman can move beyond her woundedness, she may come to new understanding of the human condition and with that to compassion for the weak and struggling persons that we all are. Such transformation does happen, and it is blessed.

We are called also to a caring for her husband. Whether it be habit and misperception of life's worthiness, or finally a physically entangling affliction, the road back from addiction is arduous and long; it requires steady commitment and recommitment. It will, at best, often be a lonely struggle, 'nobody else can do it for you.' Regeneration of the spirit may be the way through.

Unstillness comes from an ungathered soul. The tight breathing, tense smile, restless hands, vigilant posture give evidence of a poor stressed body trying to hold together impossible contradictions. Too often the knowledge of who we are, what brings us joy, our part in a greater community, eludes us.

The visitor to my office almost always blames the tension on outside forces: a demanding job, a thoughtless boss, too little money, a poor partner, an impossible schedule.

The body breaks down, but the fatigue, stomach trouble, headache, back pain, repeated infection is seen more as a betrayal than as a communication that needs to be listened to. We all yearn to be whole, yet we do not take time to learn what that could mean.

As long as the tension persists, the problems can only tighten. No person controls the universe, or even the smallest part of it, and efforts to do so only bring pain and disharmony. Without the balance of a centred spirit, the

mind whirls uselessly around, repeating over and over un-
happy events or dreaded outcomes; even relatively minor
offences bring reminiscence of early childhood hurts. Emotions, without the perspective of a wider spirit, bounce
erratically and fruitlessly, sometimes to anger, sometimes
to fear. Our feelings may be deadened finally into what has
come to be called depression. The body falters without care,
without leisure, exercise, nutrition in harmony with the
spirit.

The therapist searches for ways to bring the person
back to centredness. If for a moment, quietness, perspective, can be gained; if, even for a moment, something of
beauty, one item of nature, the simplicity of a leaf, can be
recognized, the seeker may begin to find the way back, the
way to healing.

Steps which need to be taken can be envisioned.
Clarity may form as to whether the freedom of the soul can
be found within the familiar situation, or whether, instead,
strength must be summoned to change the situation altogether. The important step is that the person find a way to
return to the centre. With encouragement and practice, the
way of healing can become familiar.

But we do not live only alone, nor are we meant to do
so. Our human task is to learn community with others on
the earth, and with community, compassion. This may be
learned first with our intimate partners or with a living
community, though this may be the most difficult. Eventually community is to be learned with our wider society, our
species, with the planet earth and with all its rich
interconnectedness.

Couples come to my office. Pain and anger, disappointment and need, expectations of a nurturance missed in childhood, economic and social pressures mix together in tears and frustration. The illusion and hubris of the first intimacies are over and the hard work of mutuality has hardly begun. Old patterns of dominance and subordination, once accepted as familiar or surreptitiously subverted, are not now tolerable in an age that is learning equality. Yet we've only begun to learn another way.

Together a quiet breath must be taken and the puzzle slowly sorted out. Each person must be listened to, each person cared for; with patience, each learns to hear both the pain and the tenderness of the other, their yearning. Though selves will still clash and needs still differ, gradually a new comprehension of relationship can be developed, a configuration of 'we' made up, now, of a cared for 'me' and a cared for 'thee.'

If enough life-affirming joy can be remembered, enough good will brought forth, a path towards community may be found, even through this complexity. This path, this concept of 'we', is a pattern for the community of all humankind. Such a pattern of relationship, embracing and caring for complexity, for diversity, for self-dependence and interdependence, can lead us all finally to wholeness.

This is the lesson of love, the saving spirit of compassion. It will be learned through generosity and warmheartedness, through an imagination which knows how another's suffering feels to them. In the deepest sense it will be an awareness of that of god in those next to us and in every other person on the earth. We will come to know this more easily as we turn ourselves more and more towards the centre.

We, therapists and those who come to us, can be patient with ourselves. 'What we would do, we do not, and that which we would not do, that we do.' Sometimes we must first accept the contradictory community within our own person. We are not simple organisms. Our selves are a mingling together of unique inborn qualities and a unique pattern of relationship, environment, frights, happinesses and tragedies. These often bring to us conflicting desires, hopes, expectations, and fears.

All of us have the task of acknowledging the diverse needs and wants within ourselves, respecting the purposes they serve, or have served, sifting them through in the light, to let go what we are ready to let go, integrating what we can, and enjoying those unexpected parts which seem true to ourselves and to our care for others and which amaze us with their expression.

The human race is blessed with expression which cannot be contained within rational expectations. Humour, art, theatre, dance, music, simple play, are evidence of this rich diversity. Great humanitarian effort may grow from unmeasurable source. Mystery and beauty are a part of god.

Psychotherapists are beginning to accept and learn from the ways the great religions have long known to call humankind back to its deep spirit. Meditation, prayer, attention to breathing, visualization: 'Whatsoever things are true, whatsoever things are honest, whatsoever things are just, whatsoever things are pure, whatsoever things are lovely, whatsoever things are of good report; if there be any

virtue and if there be any praise, think on these things.'
(Phillipians 4: 8)

Though the therapists bring more secular practices
also of biofeedback, relaxation, medication, I do not believe
that real healing will come from a quick formula or cognitive direction. It is the slow, disciplined, regular turning
and returning to the centre which holds the promise of
transformation, transformative for those who suffer and for
a world that suffers.

> There is a balm in Gilead
> To make the wounded whole.
> There is a balm in Gilead
> To heal the sin-sick world.
> (old Christian hymn)

The *Bhagavad Gita* 12.4 turns us to the healing centre:

> KRISHNA:
> Who have all the powers of the soul in harmony,
> and the same loving mind for all:
> who find joy in the good of all beings—
> they reach in truth
> my very self.

6

The Need for Holistic Medicine

RALF DAMWERTH

'The treatment of a part should not be attempted
without treatment of the entirety.'

Plato: 'The State', 380 ante Domino.

Nobody should give up the right to benefit from the
amazing skills of modern medicine. But it is good to
remember that modern medicine generally does a poor job
of assisting people with the everyday needs of managing
their physical, emotional and spiritual irregularities.

Modern medicine restricts itself only to the body, neglecting the subtle dimensions of the human personality.
According to it, life is limited to the body and chemical
pathways determine our thoughts and behaviour and are

responsible for health and illness. The body is considered a machine which can be repaired in case of disorder. Such ideas create high expectations in the patient going to a physician. These expectations are enhanced by TV reports of new breakthroughs in modern medicine. These so-called breakthroughs have not changed the limited concept of modern medicine. It continues to restrict itself to manipulations in the body, only the methods are getting finer. But the truth is that the body is only a superficial part of our real personality.

Ellis Huber, president of the Berlin medical profession, has brilliantly analysed the problems of modern medicine and the mistakes of the German health system in his book *Love Instead of Valium*. He says that because of the limited view of modern medicine, physicians often do not find a diagnosis to the complaints of their patients. What they find are symptoms. It is these symptoms that are treated. People get impressed by technical investigations, which seem to allow fascinating insight into the body. Patients want to be in good hands and be treated in places where they can be connected to a maximum number of 'unbribable' and 'objective' machines. The trouble in finding explanations makes even normal laboratory results or minimal abnormalities in X-ray a cause of the complaint.

The example of 'the hospital medicine' gives the whole picture of healthcare. Through the feudal 'superintendent system' with its steep hierarchy starting with senior physicians and down to assistants and vocational beginners, the conventional state is cemented. The superintendents make a lot of money using mostly technical equipment and generally have little contact with the patient.

Many physicians have become emotional illiterates. They have been trained only in 'body medicine.' Their desire to conquer diseases often makes them blind. They do not recognize that the battlefield they are fighting on is a human being.

The lack of sympathetic understanding and the impressive equipment are what institutionalized medicare offer patients today. Our medicine has trained people to hand over their responsibility to the doctor.

The so-called scientific medicine must do away with two things. One, the belief in 'objectiveness' and, two, the conviction that further biomedical and biochemical procedures will control all diseases of human beings. We must realize that only the widening of medical perspective can open up new possibilities.

What Is Holistic Medicine?

Holistic medicine has become a vogue word in recent years. But what does it really mean? Wholeness is more than the sum of its parts, because a part is meaningful only in the context of the wholeness. The well-known Indian story of six blind men trying to describe an elephant illustrates that. The holistic medical approach is to see and treat a human being as a unity of body, mind and soul. Holistic medicine is not here to replace conventional medicine but to improve it and to open up new dimensions. The physical illness of a human being is not to be considered as something isolated but as a disorder of the total human being, a disorder which must be recognized and treated at all levels. Holistic physicians help patients attain greater self-responsibility in maintaining health. Instead of being 'a half-god in white,' the physician becomes a friend in daily life.

Holistic Medicine Gives Disease a Deeper Meaning

The picture of a body which can be repaired as a machine is so tempting because real and active confrontation with the true problem is thus avoided. Ellis Huber writes: 'Children have already learned in their families how to "solve" little problems with tablets. Small children swallow painkillers, and nobody is asking, of which origin they are.'

Many people ask: 'If God really exists, why does he burden us with diseases and limitations?' Just as every child grows up through some painful experiences and gradually gains the wisdom of an adult, in the same way the embryonic consciousness matures through limitations and suffering. Vivekananda says: 'Analyse yourselves and you will find that every blow you received came to you because you prepared yourselves for it.' Buddha said: 'Look on your present life, then you will know what you have done in the past. Look on your present actions and you will know how you will be in the future.' Disease therefore has this benefit: it shows us the mistakes we made. Pain and suffering are nothing more then alarm-signals.

Holistic Medicine Emphasizes Prevention

To prevent diseases is an important matter in holistic medicine. It advocates healthy food and good diet, physical exercises and, in general, a natural and ecological life-style.

To develop good habits is absolutely necessary for good health.

Concerning prevention of disease, we can learn a lot from Asian cultures. Hatha Yoga, for example, is a brilliant system of maintaining the body and detecting any dysfunction very early.

Prevention also means to work early on conflicts and the tasks of life. Many diseases begin on the mental plane and therefore they can be recognized earliest there. Here a spiritual upbringing can be most helpful.

Holistic Medicine Concentrates on Health

Often people who want to be healed concentrate more on the possible bad effects of the disease than on the possible healing. Through that the disease becomes not only a physical but also a mental problem. Many physicians see not the human being in the patient but only the 'gastric ulcer of room no.13' and, when they go round the wards, they ask the patients only about their complaints. It would be so much more beneficial to divert the patient from his or her complaints! A room can be illuminated at once if light is let in, but not if one tries to drive it out.

Holistic Medicine Aims at Self-healing

It takes two to practise holistic medicine, the physician *and* the patient. Everything cannot be left in the hands of the physician. The patient also has to take part in his or her own recovery. The physician can at best be a therapeutic partner and guide. The effort of the patient is decisive for recovery and healing. A very important role in natural medicine is played by the power of self-healing. Holistic medicine tries to strengthen this power on the physical and mental levels.

Vivekananda says: 'Strength is life, weakness is death.' Faith, will-power and imagination are the instruments for conquering diseases. That is why it is so important to strengthen the patient's faith that healing is possible, even when he or she makes very little progress. It is the faith and not the time that determines when healing will take place. Even the inevitable death due to an 'unhealable disease' should not lead a person astray from his faith in healing. In such situations, spiritual people meditate on God, seeking freedom not from disease but from the body itself.

Holistic Medicine Accepts Death and Dying

Death is no longer failure of medicine but a natural event. Death means change. Changes accompany our whole life and they are often combined with anxiety. If we want to live, we must accept the reality of death. An important task of the new medicine is to free us from the anxiety concerning death. This it does by encouraging us to lead a meaningful life. Holistic medicine tries to create an atmosphere for the dying, in which the patient can let go of everything and die peacefully with dignity.

Healthcare System in Germany

There is limited amount of money in the German healthcare system. And the amount is determined by politicians and society. There are about 300,000 physicians in Germany, and only a part of these, who are panel-doctors, decide how the money is spent.

Intensive care and costly investigations give physicians the feeling of importance; for the patient, it means fatter medical bills and often no special benefit. Most physicians follow this simple method: get to know the symptons, give the problem a name, and offer a pharmacologic solution. This has a great advantage in the existing healthcare system: more patients per hour can be seen by prescription than by long conversations.

About 5 billion DM (1 DM is about 18 Indian rupees) are wasted for remedies which are never taken. 6 billion DM are spent on remedies whose healing powers are doubtful. An unbelievable mismanagement! And the pharmaceutic industry always finds new ways to make physicians prescribe their products. A lot of money is needlessly spent on the inflated administrative structures of hospitals and other medical institutions.

People in Germany long for holistic medicine. Homeopathy and Acupuncture are among the favourites here in alternative medicine.

If we optimize the healthcare system in Germany, more than 100,000 physician jobs can be arranged for a more 'conversation-oriented' medicine. The healthcare system must become a 'non-profit concern' which focuses on the health of every individual and of society.

Holistic medicine can have a good financial backing if politicians and the established medical profession change their attitudes. But this is a process that will take time. The healthcare system of the future is a net of institutions that supports everyone in being self-responsible about health, it will support people in their personal development; it will remove the separation between medicine, psychology and religion, and it will become an important instrument for the evolution of society.

7

Listening to the Body's Inner Voice

CARLA MARTINEZ

'The will of God will never lead you where the grace of God cannot keep you.' I live by these words. And though I did not know them when I was being diagnosed with a life-threatening illness in 1988, somewhere inside my heart I was listening within the quiet.

That day in April I sat in the doctor's office filled with exhaustion from whatever it was my body was carrying in pain. What I learned from this man with a gentle presence and concerned voice was that I had a disease called scleroderma. My immune system was attacking itself and had begun producing too much collagen throughout my body. What this meant was that the skin and everything else collagen touches would tighten and become hard. Well, collagen is everywhere in the body, so this included the vital organs. I asked the doctor what the prognosis of this illness was and he responded by saying, 'You will die.' I asked him how this would happen, and he said that when the collagen sclerosed around the vital organs, there was nothing more he could do to help me and I would die, that is the way of this disease. I believe my healing began in that instant, because it was then I closed my eyes and saw every organ functioning perfectly. Then I asked Spirit if I would die and was told No, but that it would get worse before it got better and I would need to prepare for this time. I am glad I listened.

Looking back to this important day in my life I realize that the first ten minutes with a doctor or other healthcare practitioner who is diagnosing a state of health for us is the most crucial time of our healing. It is in this time we shape our own attitude towards illness, health and healing. How the news of our health is reported to us is important; however, what is more important is how we receive the information, and then what we do with it. Granted, here in America we grow up assuming doctors have all the answers regarding our health. But who knows the body better than the one living in it? Certainly, doctors are highly trained to help us heal on a physical level, but are they skilled in assisting us with the wholeness of our being—the body, mind, and spirit? Some of them are, but we must take responsibility and learn to feel what our body is doing and listen to what it is saying when we become injured or ill. This takes practice.

I have had many years of practice. Without going into specifics, I have had two eye surgeries, two leg surgeries,

back surgery and brain surgery all before the age of thirty.
I was in a car accident which nearly killed me. The brain
surgery was for a tumor which doctors didn't think I would
survive. Pulmonary edema, which can be fatal, was a
precursor symptom to scleroderma, and then there was
scleroderma. By the age of thirty-two I had had four life-
threatening experiences! I see all of these experiences as
gifts, wake up calls, if you will. Sometimes I ask myself,
'What took me so long to hear the song of life?' Finally,
through all of these painful and often debilitating experiences, I have learned that illness and injury have great
things to teach us. Finally, I am listening. Finally, I am
paying attention!

     And pay attention we must, if we are to move through
illness and injury to wellness. In my many encounters on
the path of healing and wellness, there has been much to
which I have had to give attention. There was the illness or
injury itself and what needed to be learned. There was
physical limitation, diet, medicines to promote healing and
eliminate pain ranging from natural homeopathic remedies
to prescription pharmaceuticals. There were many different
modalities to utilize: chiropractic, acupuncture, Therapeutic
Touch, massage, vitamins, herbs, physical therapy, yoga,
meditation, visualization and other spiritual work to be
practised. You name it, I probably discovered it in the process of my healing. You see, from my perspective, when one
is in a life-threatening situation and wants to heal, one will
do whatever it takes to do so. I ran the gamut between
conventional and holistic modalities. The most unconven-
tional thing I did was subject myself to bee-venom therapy
for six weeks. You might wonder why I would subject

myself to such a horrific experience. Because I was dealing with a life-threatening situation, I was willing to try anything that would not endanger my well being. Bee-venom is purported to have a property in it that helps bring the immune system back into balance. That is what I wanted: my immune system back in balance. I was in remission from scleroderma, but that wasn't enough for me. I wanted it gone, out of my body completely. Even though it was extremely painful, subjecting myself to bee stings proved to serve me well. After six weeks of getting stung by bees three days a week, working my way from three stings a session to fourteen stings a session, and a serious staph-infection, scleroderma was gone. And for six years it has been so!

People will ask me what I think it was that healed me. The truth is I believed I would get well. Given that, I learned to trust in the guidance of Spirit in my life. Granted, I had many opportunities over the years to learn to trust, but somehow, the lessons didn't stay with me, and it was the gift of scleroderma and a doctor saying 'you will die' that taught me to pay attention and trust. Still, over the years, I can see how the ability to trust progressed in my healing process. Yes, I would listen to doctors tell me how they could and could not help me, but having had so many exchanges with many different healthcare practitioners I learned to ask questions and do research about the particular illness or injury I was experiencing at the time. I believe that when we are in the care of another we mustn't place full responsibility on that individual to 'make us well.' It is imperative that we take responsibility for our own healing and learn everything we can about the illness or injury, and if we have questions or concerns about any aspect of our healing process, we must not hesitate to ask our doctor or practitioner. They may not have all the answers to our questions, but they can provide us with insight and understanding to what we do not know about our bodies. They can be guides for us along our healing path. They will listen well to us to the extent that we will listen well to them. Through the many years in the practice of healing that I have had, this has been my experience.

In the event a doctor or practitioner believes there is no cure for a given disease, it is still imperative to have their support. Even in the midst of a life-threatening illness they can support us. During the time of scleroderma I had a couple of experiences where practitioners gave up on my ability to heal. I immediately released them from my care. If I believe I can be healed, I want the people around me to believe it too. It's that simple. It isn't necessary for me to try to convince anybody about my healing, but it is necessary to have people around me who can support and guide me in it. I suggest to anyone who is focused on their healing to keep this in mind, because those who cannot support us on our healing path can only weigh us down. We need to be lifted. Healing lifts us to a higher place.

Healing takes place on all levels of our being—physical, mental, emotional, and spiritual. We cannot separate one from the other, and yet, I remember being so focused on my physical survival at certain times in my life that I shut down my ability to feel emotionally. As a way to endure the physical pain I became stoic. For a long time I didn't allow myself to cry or be angry or sad or feel any of the other emotions such as loss and grieving which accompany debilitating illness and injury. All I understood was that there was work in front of me to do in order to stay alive. My mind was focused on the tactics of basic physical survival. But how alive was I, really, when I wasn't able to feel?

Years later I see how the ability to close off my feelings served me in the only way possible at that time. Somehow something in us knows exactly what to do and when to do it. Throughout my healing I listened to my body's inner voice and discovered that I always knew exactly what to do and when to do it. Timing was everything. My doctors and practitioners were my guides and allies on the journey.

I understand now how we can only take on so much at any given time. Again, 'The will of God will never lead you where the grace of God cannot keep you.' To me, this is one of the spiritual laws of the universe. It was after the threat of scleroderma and I became well, again, that I discovered this *spirit-changing* quote at the Vedanta Temple in Santa Barbara, California. Fully understanding its import, I wept. I knew I had been completely guided and comforted by the way of Spirit in my life. Everything I had ever done had led me to this place. At last, I am paying attention and have learned to trust in the motion of Spirit in my life.

8
An Appointment with Life

SAM GRACI

On November 3, 1995, the American space agency, NASA, released a series of stunning photographs captured from the ends of the known universe, by the Hubble Space Telescope. These pictures are not only scientifically significant, but breathtakingly beautiful as well.

In these pictures we see great towering thunderheads, billowing high into the evening sky as they catch the last illuminating rays of the setting sun. They are so startlingly three dimensional, so sharp, that the mind wants to domesticate them, to bring them down to our known earth, to imagine them rising on the horizon, just beyond some distant mountains at sunset.

These are no ordinary clouds. They are not 30,000 feet high but almost 6 trillion miles high. They are not illuminated with ordinary earthly light but with searing ultraviolet radiation spewing from nuclear fires at the centre of a handful of newly formed stars. They are 7,000 light-years from earth—more than 400 million times as far away as the sun is from the earth.

This cosmic vista of momentous sights can stir anybody's imagination. These pictures are rare glimpses of the outer boundaries of physical reality and the fiery stew in which nature perpetually regenerates itself.

Galactic Collisions Create

A small galaxy smashed through the centre of the graceful spiral shaped Cartwheel Galaxy. With incomparable power, the impact sent a shock wave speeding outward at 200,000 m.p.h., forcefully pushing gas and dust in front of it. The debris caught up in this galactic stew was compressed and ignited into billions of new stars. Shock waves of gas (protected as if in a mother's womb) ejecting from stars, plow into surrounding gasses at nearly 200,000 m.p.h. A similar and violent event probably accompanied the creation of our own sun and its solar system some 5 billion years ago.

The Incredible Cosmic Creature

The newborn baby embodies innocence yet conceals the most taunting of all riddles: the generation of human life. The story begins with the sperm and egg colliding, then they combine to form a single cell. Sheltered in the mother's womb, the cell multiplies. Soon there are hundreds of different cells able to make some 50,000 different proteins to control the work of all our cells—collagen to build skin, insulin to control energy use, hemoglobin to supply oxygen.

Before long, the groups of cells are forming into layers, then into sheets and tubes, sliding into the proper place at the proper time, forming an eye exactly where an eye should be, the heart where the heart belongs. The order of appearance is precise, with structures like nerves and veins appearing just in time to support the forming organs that will soon appear.

Eventually the cosmic creature is formed. During a day in a city such as New York, Tokyo or Calcutta, the average adult inhales some 20–25 billion particles of foreign matter, yet the respiratory tract delivers to the lungs air that is virtually free of debris.

Why Life Is So Precious

We are special because we are integral parts of Infinity. Within our bodies course the same elements that flame in the stars. Whether the story of life is told by a theologian who believes that creation is an act of God, or by scientists who theorize that it was a consequence of chemistry and physics, the result is the same; the stuff of stars has come alive. Inanimate chemicals have turned into living things that breathe, swallow, talk, blossom, think, imagine, write, dream, and teach.

The living beings of earth are cosmic creatures, products of celestial events—atomic collisions, stellar explosions, molecular unions—that were cataclysmic yet fortuitous. We are children of the universe.

Only those that can elaborate survive. Evolution accumulates the successful. Evolution is addition or subtraction—reproduction with a garnish. In the words of physiologist Walter Cannon, 'the wisdom of the body is among the most precise of selective refinements.' This wisdom is apparent to some degree in every living organism.

Billions of years, changes, deaths, and lives have created a remarkable self-adjusting balance called homeostasis. By this process, biological mechanisms work in unison to protect the body's internal stability from the ongoing threats of nature. These forces automatically activate, some within a fraction of a second, some more slowly. If a man hemorrhages, his body pulls water from tissues into the circulatory system, this keeps blood pressure from dropping below critical levels. When a woman is suffering frostbite, her body has automatically adjusted by slowing the blood flow to her toes and fingers, ears and nose, reserving heat and oxygen for the all-important brain and the organs in her chest and abdomen. As an insect approaches our eye, we blink.

This internal equilibrium can adapt itself to a temperature change of even a fraction of a degree, bathing the body in cooling perspiration when it becomes too warm, and when cold, prompting shivers to convert energy to heat.

Alliance Develops—Aggression Competes

Once people said that natural selection favoured the most aggressive animals, those dripping red from their tooth and claw by devouring their competitors. But ages of mutations have produced many species that flourish because of alliance rather than aggression. The human mother who perishes to protect her offspring, the meditative holy person, the deeply pondering grandparent, this now lives in the genes of the future family.

One of the most intricate of life's creations is the human brain. By the strength of thought and hope rather than muscle—humans lifted the lineage of life to the capacities to love, to cherish, to ponder, to succor, to guarantee the future of the species not just by proliferation, but by nurture and wisdom. Some genes promote aggression in humans, while others are the product of and likewise encourage creative realization by a process of alliance.

Who Are We

These evolutionary origins do not diminish us, they exalt us. With our human bodies—biological galaxies of stellar dust—we are not only the centre of the universe, we are more. We are the universe. We are its nuclei, its electrons, its atoms, combining and recombining, we are its past and we are its future. Ultimately, we are not an individual limited to a singular identity but rather Infinite, ever-present and eternal. We all are the intimate cosmic dance, call it God, the Divine Mother or Being. Now we have a choice how to feed or, more specifically, how to fuel these bodies whose origin is eternity itself and whose purpose is Being and Becoming.

High Octane Fuels

We have both a responsibility and a practical necessity to feed our bodies with simple, natural foods that are high octane fuels for the design and functioning of this remarkable organism.

High octane fuels are clean water fruits, vegetables, sea vegetables, whole grains, herbs and their teas, seeds, nuts, legumes, and plain white yogurt without fruit or sweeteners.

Low octane fuels are all sugars (glucose, sucrose, fructose), excess oils, fried foods, alcohols, stimulants such as narcotics, tea and coffee, white breads, candies, carbonated soft drinks, and sweetened fruit juices.

Science has discovered the presence of phytochemicals ('phyto' is a Greek prefix meaning 'plant derived') that are disease-preventing (i.e. cancer-preventing) substances in all fruits and vegetables. Eat a variety of coloured fruits and vegetables to get a full range of phytochemicals. You must favour the consumption of no, or fewer, animal protein foods and dairy, but recognize that some people need modest but regular amounts of animal protein.

The human body has developed into an organism designed to be vegetarian in food choice. It is imperative we consume a diet that is 75% alkaline ash and only 25% acid ash by weight. This is the single most critical point in maintaining superior good health and a calmer disposition. Discover the magic and grandeur of ordinary existence by eating simple foods, chewed well with some raw vegetables and fresh fruits daily.

All cosmic reactions in the universe depend upon available fuels. Likewise, our bodies, truly cosmic bodies, require simple, natural foods for chemical reactions that maintain it at a level of optimal health and homeostasis. We must not let taste buds, cultural influences and

emotions dictate our fuels but an understanding of the lofti-
ness of our origin and the necessity of our maintenance, so
we may honour our appointment with life.

I would like to end with 15 STEPS TO LIVING HEALTHIER ...
NOW!

15 Steps to Living Healthier . . . Now!

1. Eat as if your life depended upon it. Our cosmic origin
   requires high octane fuels.
2. Chew foods well to begin the process of digestion.
3. Leave stomach 20% empty for digestion, discover the
   benefits of calorie restriction.
4. Combine foods properly for assimilation.
5. Consume 8–12 glasses of quality water daily but not
   with meals. Drink water from a closed container with a
   straw.
6. Diet should be 75% alkaline ash-forming foods and 25%
   acid-forming foods. This is very critical.
7. Consume organically grown fruits and vegetables when
   possible. Avoid chemically laden and over-processed
   foods in cans or boxes.
8. Consume enzymatically alive foods full of organic
   water, various colours, as well as phytochemicals and
   antioxidants. Eat 6 servings of vegetables, three of fruit
   daily. Do not overcook vegetables.
9. Reinoculate the colon by eating plain, unsweetened yogurt daily.
10. Keep the colon clean.
11. Take time to breathe deeply. Reduce stress naturally.
    Rejoice in life.

12. Sleep sufficiently for your needs and exercise daily.
13. Expose your skin and eyes to sunlight daily, at only the appropriate times, avoid burns, never look at the sun directly.
14. Reach out with love and compassion to others and see them as your own. Do not criticize.
15. Meditate and pray to calm our bodies and minds, think good thoughts, do right actions, be truthful in speech. Smile, it is magical.

AVOID

Excess protein, alcohol, sugars, excess salt, overly processed foods, tobacco, tea, carbonated beverages, margarine, coffee, refined foods, electrical power lines, hydrogenated or rancid oils, fried foods, sweetened foods.

REMEMBER

OUR HEALTH IS GAINED OR LOST AT
THE CELLULAR LEVEL DAILY !

9

Energy Foods for Radiant Health—
Get Energized!

ELVIRA GRACI

A cid runs batteries, not bodies. As you read these words, your body is generating acid and you are eliminating acid. No need to worry, all your cells produce acid as they function, and your lungs eliminate these acids every time you exhale. The acid your body produces is relatively weak and usually does not cause any problems. On the other hand, the excess acids your body gets from eating too much protein, grains, sugar, dairy, by strenuous exercise or excess stress, causes a lot of serious problems and must be excreted in the urine.

Dynamic Health

You need to know more about the relationship between food and total optimum health. The acid level in your body may be the major factor in determining your level of health. When a log is burned in your fireplace it leaves an ash. When any food is eaten, after it is digested, it also leaves an ash in the body. Foods either leave an acid ash or an alkaline ash. Optimum health is in an alkaline body. The average 20th century diet, life-style, stress, pace and environment produce far more acid than is healthy. Your body is alkaline by design but acidic by function. This means that your body's dynamic, optimum health is dependent upon it being alkaline.

My personal research has indicated that 90% of our general population is far too acidic, which leads to a variety of negative health effects. Over time, being too acidic is the beginning of degenerative disease and aging. Immediately, being too acidic causes you to feel energyless, mentally exhausted and for your skin and hair to lose their shine and radiant appearance.

Acid-Alkaline Balance—Key Indicator of Health

True health is thus dependent on the acid-alkaline balance. If the body is out of balance, the result is excessive stress on your body tissues. Inevitably this leads to disease. The effects of being too acidic are:

*free radical oxidation occurs with greater ease, while antioxidant activity is impaired.

*vitamins and minerals from foods or supplements are not absorbed well.

*friendly bacteria in the small intestines die and the immune system is impaired.

*connective tissue becomes weakened and your facial skin and hair lose their tone.

*sleep patterns are disturbed.

*you become physically and mentally exhausted mid-afternoon and in the evening.

*colds, infections, headaches and flus are much more common.

*you become impatient and lose your calmness more easily . . . you get 'burned out.'

A person is rarely too alkaline. Generally it would be a vegan consuming no or too little protein.

Eat Your Way to Good Health

In general, vegetables, fruits (preferably organically grown), sea vegetables (algae), herbs and quality water yield an alkaline ash while grains, vegetarian or animal protein, dairy, sugar and oils yield an acid ash. Notable exceptions are cranberries which leave a strong acid ash, and both millet and organic plain yogurt which leave a mildly alkaline ash.

The general rule is that you should consume 75% of your food daily, by weight, from the alkaline ash-forming foods and 25% from the acid ash-forming foods. The average

1990s diet has reversed these numbers and correspond-
ingly, degenerative diseases are afflicting more people at a
younger age and their numbers are rising.

pH Indicates Acidity or Alkalinity

Your pH indicates acidity or alkalinity and how
healthy you are. The pH of fluids in your body doesn't stay

continued on p. 102

EFFECT OF FOODS ON BODY CHEMISTRY
A RECIPE FOR LIFE
NOTE

The Chart on the next two pages provides information
which gives an indication of the contribution of various food
substances to the acidity or alkalinity of the body fluids
and, ultimately, to the urine, saliva and venous blood.

The kidneys help to maintain the neutrality of the
body fluids by excreting the excess acid or alkali in the
urine.

In general, it is important to eat a diet which contains
foods from both sides of the chart.

Allergic reactions and other forms of stress tend to
produce acids in the body. The presence of high acidity indicates that more of your foods should be selected from the
alkaline forming group.

You may find it useful to check your urine pH using
nitrazine paper in order to find out if your food selection is
providing the desired balance. Check urine pH 3x/day.

A urine pH of between 6.2 in the morning and 7.4 in
the afternoon is ideal, but it will vary over the day depending upon the foods you eat as well as allergic reactions and
other stress factors.

People vary, but for most, the ideal diet is
75% Alkaline and 25% Acid Ash Forming Foods.

ALKALINE ASH FORMING FOODS

VEGETABLES
Garlic
Asparagus
Fermented Veggies
Water Cress
Beets
Broccoli
Brussel Sprouts
Cabbage
Carrots
Cauliflower
Celery
Chard
Chlocella (Algae)
Colland Greens
Cucumber
* Eggplant
Kale
Kohlrabi
Lettuces
Mushrooms
Mustard Greens
Nova Scotia Dulse
Dandelions
Edible Flowers
Onions
Parsnips
Peas
* Peppers
* Potatoes
Pumpkin
Rutabaga
Sea Veggies
Spirulina (algae)
Sprouts (all types)
Squashes
Alfalfa Grass
Barley Grass
Wheat Grass
Wild Greens

* Nightshade veggies

NOTE: Use organically grown whenever possible.

BEVERAGES
Green Drinks
Veggie Juices
Coffee (black)
Fresh Fruit Juice (unsweetened)
Organic Milk (unpasteurized)
Mineral Water (noncarbonated)
Quality Water

NUTS & SEEDS
Almonds
Chestnuts
Coconut
Flax Seeds
Pumpkin Seeds
Sesame Seeds
Squash Seeds
Sunflower Seeds
Millet
Sprouted Seeds, Nuts

SWEETENERS
Honey, Raw
Molasses, Raw

SPICES & SEASONINGS
Cinnamon
Curry
Ginger
Mustard
Chili Peppers
Salt (Sea, Celtic)
Miso
Tamari
All Herbs

ORIENTAL VEGETABLES
Maitake
Daikon
Dandelion Root
Shiitake
Kombu
Reishi
Nori
Umeboshi
Wakame

FRUITS
Apples
Apricots
Avocado
Bananas
Blackberry
Blueberry
Cantaloupe
Cherries
Currants
Dates
Figs
Grapes, Raisins
Grapefruits
Honeydew
Lemons
Limes
Nectarines
Oranges
Peaches
Pears
Pineapple
Raspberry (berries)
Rhubarb
Strawberries
Tangerine
* Tomatoes
Tropical Fruits
Watermelon

TEAS
Green Tea
Herbal Teas
Dandelion Tea
Ginseng
Banchi Tea
Kombucha

OTHER
Apple cider vinegar
Bee Pollen
Lecithin Granules
Dairy-free probiotic Cultures
Organic Yogurt

ACID ASH FORMING FOODS

FATS & OILS

Avocado Oil
Canola Oil
Corn Oil
Hemp Seed Oil
Flax Oil
Grape Seed Oil
Lard
Olive Oil
Safflower Oil
Sesame Oil
Sunflower Oil

FRUITS

Cranberries

GRAINS

Amaranth
Barley
Buckwheat
Corn
Oats (rolled)
Quinoa
Rice (brown,
Basmati)
Rye
Spelt
Kamut
Wheat
Hemp Seed Flour

DAIRY
PRODUCTS

Whey Protein
Cheese, Cow
Cheese, Goat
Cheese, Processed
Cheese, Sheep
Milk (avoid BGH)

NUTS & BUTTERS

Cashews
Filberts
Brazil Nuts
Peanuts
Peanut Butter
Pecans
Tahini
Walnuts

ANIMAL PROTEIN

Beef
Carp
Chicken
Clams
Duck
Eel
Eggs
Fish, White Meat
Lamb
Lobster
Mussels
Oyster
Pork
Rabbit
Salmon
Shrimp
Scallops
Tuna
Turkey
Venison

PASTA

Noodles
Macaroni
Spaghetti

OTHER

Distilled Vinegar
Brewers Yeast
Wheat Germ

DRUGS & CHEMICALS

Chemicals,
Drugs, Medicinal
Drugs, Psychedelics
Pesticides,
Herbicides

SWEETS & SWEETENERS

Candy
Honey
Maple Syrup
Saccharin
Soft Drinks
Sugar

ALCOHOLIC BEVERAGES

Beer
Spirits
Vodka, etc.
Whiskey, Etc.
Wine

BEANS & LEGUMES

Black Beans
Chick Peas
Green Peas
Kidney Beans
Lentils
Lima Beans
Pinto Beans
Red Beans
Soybeans
Soy Products
Soy Milk
Tofu
White Beans
Rice Milk
Almond Milk

constant; it fluctuates according to your stress level, sleep patterns, exercise level and especially your diet. The term pH stands for 'potential of Hydrogen'—it is a measure of the relative acidity or alkalinity of a solution. The scale of pH runs from 1 to 14. Zero is total acidic and 14 totally alkaline. The middle of this line is 7, neutral. Quality water has a pH of 7 and ideally so should you.

Your Body Is Alkaline

All of the fluids of the body, with the exception of those in the stomach, are—or should be—alkaline. You can check your pH by monitoring your urine, saliva or venous blood. For practical reasons I recommend you test your urine pH three times a day at 7:00 a.m., 3:00 p.m. and 9:00 p.m. Chart or graph the pH of your urine for 30 days to get an accurate measure of your state of health. Use nitrazine paper (by Bristol-Myers Squibb) or pHydrion papers (by Micro Essential Labs) available at your favourite health food store or pharmacy. They come in rolls with a colour chart and pH rating. Simply rip off a one inch piece and put it in mid-stream urine collected in a disposable paper cup. The paper strip will turn a colour that you match to a number on the graph.

A Healthy pH

Your ideal urine pH should be between 6.2–7.0 at 7:00 a.m., 6.6–7.0 at 3:00 p.m. and 7.0–7.4 at 9:00 p.m. The pH is not static but fluid and naturally cycles through the day. If you have been consuming an incorrect balance and your diet has been more than 25% acid ash-forming foods, your body chemistry has been impaired and operating at less than optimal. Your body wants to protect itself at all times, so if the diet is too acidic, your kidneys dump ammonia into your system to balance all the acids. Ammonia is very alkaline. Ammonia as a urine neutralizer (balances the acids) is an emergency backup system to take care of an emergency and dangerous situation, as the strong acids can burn out your internal tissues. Therefore, if your urine has an ammonia smell or your pH is 7.5–8.0 or more at each testing, assume your body chemistry is too acidic and you have ammonia in your urine to help reduce those strong and corrosive acids. This is a critical warning to begin to eat a more alkaline ash diet immediately.

A Recipe for Life

We must consume both alkaline and acid ash foods daily—both are necessary. The acids from proteins, grains and dairy are easily buffered (neutralized) by the organic minerals found primarily in live, enzyme-rich foods such as vegetables, fruits, water, all herbs and sea vegetables. To maintain a sufficient alkaline reserve (organic mineral reserve) so you can buffer these acid ash-forming foods, it is imperative you consume a diet that is 75% alkaline ash-forming foods daily. Eat some raw foods, be it fruits, vegetables (juices of both), seeds, salads, raw nuts, sea veggies, fermented veggies, grated veggies or herbal garnishes at each meal. Note that citrus fruits taste 'acidic' and are for the first hour in the body, but do leave an alkaline ash. Therefore I always promote you squeeze fresh lemon or lime juice (use one full lemon in 24 hours) in your

8–12 glasses of water daily. Avocados and tomatoes are fruits that can be used as vegetables. In the expansive (yin-ness) and contractive (yang-ness) theories, a diet of 75% alkaline ash foods would be ideal. Prayer, meditation, hatha yoga, Tai Chi, reflexology, massage, therapeutic touch, calming music, sitting in nature, reaching out to others with love and compassion are each human activities that buffer the acids of daily living and promote an alkaline body.

The effects of being alkaline are: (a) we are calm; (b) we have robust energy; (c) our sleep patterns are deep; (d) we have fewer colds and flus; (e) the immune system is strong to ward off disease; (f) the body has good digestion, absorption/ elimination.

The effects of being too acidic are: (a) we become flustered and agitated more quickly; (b) we become physically and mentally exhausted by mid-afternoon; (c) we do not experience deep sleep patterns; (d) we have several colds and flus each year; (e) the immune system is compromised and operating at less than optimal; (f) digestion is impaired and we experience flatulence, bloating and discomfort after meals.

Mother Nature prepares the best foods for these human bodies, and it is your choice how or if you will eat them. Appetites are learned and we must consciously and conscientiously see the Intelligence Within. The Divine Blueprint that created these powerful, natural foods.

Be natural, eat simple, eat the 'common man's' diet and avoid packaged, sweetened, canned foods that might taste good, but are thieves that rob you of your natural vibrant health.

10
Cancer, Body and Mind

PEEYUSH K. LALA

The word 'cancer' is derived from its Latin precursor 'cancrum' or the crab, to convey the notion that it 'eats away' into the normal healthy tissues leading to their destruction, and eventually the demise of the host. For centuries, the very word 'cancer', both in the West as well as in the East, has been conceived as dreadful, and sometimes even shameful, so that a patient and the family have both borne inordinate psychological pain, primarily because of sheer ignorance. Nowadays, certain cancers are curable when diagnosed early. Furthermore, public education as well as variety of social support systems services available in most of the Western countries have made the disease, even when incurable, far more bearable and manageable with dignity and courage.

Cancer is a very old disease, as old as the existence of the human race and its parental races. It is also present in other animal forms, and exists even in the plant kingdom as the more benign tumour-like growths known as 'galls'. The disease has been noted in fossilized animal remains and has been documented in various ways in the older medical literature of the West as well as the East (including the Ayurveda, which appears to provide the oldest documentation). Many feel that the incidence of cancer has been on the rise during the recent century owing to tampering of the environment by the human race. However, much of this rise is readily explained by the following fact: because of better preventive medicine (including vaccinations which have controlled most infectious diseases), human longevity has increased dramatically throughout the world. Thus there has been a concomitant unmasking of many cancers which affect older people, particularly after middle age. As will be explained later, the longer we live, the higher is our probability of developing cancer.

There are three important facts about cancer. First, it is a genetic disease; that is, cancer results from genetic changes in the normal cells of our body. Second, cancer is a 'monoclonal' disease to start with. That is, a cancer arises initially by multiplication of a single cell which has become abnormal due to genetic changes, so that all the members in the progeny are also abnormal. However, genes in cancer cells are more unstable than normal cells, so that the cancer cell population soon becomes heterogeneous due to additional genetic changes which may be different in different member cells. Third, alteration of a single gene in a normal cell seldom makes it cancerous. Usually further genetic changes are needed to make the cell behave in a grossly abnormal manner, the hallmark of cancer.

We can compare the development of cancer within the body to the development of an evil organization of gangsters within an otherwise orderly society. In an orderly society, there is division of labour and skill amongst its members contributing to the overall welfare of the society. This is also true for the healthy human body, the health depending fully on the well-organized functions of cells in various tissues which are interdependent. Cells of the heart muscle continue twitching rhythmically without rest, so that the heart can provide blood, the source of nourishment and oxygen, to all the cells in the body. Cells lining the intestine are born continuously from the underlying 'stem' cells or mother cells and mature to provide the functions of secreting enzymes to break down food particles as well as absorbing the food breakdown products to nourish the body. Ultimately the mature cells die within 3–4 days and are shed in the lumen of the intestine after their duties are over. They are then replaced by younger cells to take over their function. Similarly, our blood cells are born within the bone marrow, enter the blood when they are functionally mature, and carry on their functions for a fixed time until they wear out and die. For example, red blood cells, on the average, live for 120 days, and carry on their function of providing oxygen to other cells. White blood cells, which fight foreign invaders such as bacteria, live only for a few days. To make sure that there is a continuous production of red and white blood cells, their 'stem' cells or mother cells within the bone marrow have to remain virtually immortal, at least for the life of the individual. This is the story of normal cells within the society of a normal healthy human body.

What about cancer cells? Cancer cells are different from normal cells in many ways, although they have been derived from altered normal cells. First, they behave like the cells in our embryonic life, when cells multiply rapidly and invade tissue barriers to go to their destinations. Second, many of the cancer cells assume the properties of 'stem' cells, so that these mother cells in a cancer go on dividing and living indefinitely, that is to say, displaying immortality, provided they are nourished adequately. Third, they defy the orders of the society, that is, the molecular signals which prevent unlimited multiplication of normal cells and allow normal cells to mature. Thus cancer cells often remain immature. They not only fail to contribute to the normal functions expected of mature normal cells, but also acquire the ability of making products which are harmful to the body. Because of genetic alterations, they can either produce normal molecules such as hormones in excess, or produce abnormal molecules which are detrimental to the body. Often, like embryonic cells, they can invade neighbouring tissues. In essence, these cells live in our body as harmful parasites not only depleting the nutritional supply to normal cells but also damaging or even destroying normal cells.

Biology of Cancer Progression

As mentioned earlier, alteration of a single gene in a normal cell does not necessarily make it cancerous. It does, however, make the cell highly susceptible to becoming cancerous. A large number of cancer susceptibility genes have been identified, some of them are altered normal genes essential for a variety of cellular functions, and are given the name 'oncogene'. Similarly, there are a good number of genes which act as gatekeepers or controlling agents of certain cellular processes such as multiplication, required for the orderly function of the tissues. Disorderly behaviour such as uncontrolled cell multiplication can ensue if these genes are altered or lost by cells, a phenomenon that underlies the development of many cancers. These genes are called 'tumour-suppressors genes.' Activation of an oncogene and/or loss/alteration of a tumour suppressor gene is/are often the first recognizable genetic event(s) in the pathway that makes a normal cell eventually cancerous. Either of these events can lead to cancer susceptibility.

In certain cancers which are hereditary (a very small proportion of all cancers taken together), acquisition of cancer susceptibility can be inherited from either parent, because the abnormal gene remains in the germ line, although it may not necessarily have given rise to cancer in either parent. This is why we see certain familial forms of cancer clustered in close members of the family, for example, a small proportion of breast cancer in the female, and colon cancer in the male. In an aggressive cancer known as retinoblastoma (a cancer of the retina of the eyeball), when the altered retinoblastoma gene is inherited in the germ line, certain individuals may even be born with a cancer in the eyeball. A screening for some of these inheritable cancer susceptibility genes can now be made by highly specialized genetic laboratories. This has been a blessing in a very small proportion of cases where certain preventive measures are available to the family. In other cases, it has introduced more stress to the family which may view this as a time bomb, since preventive measures do not exist at present in such cases; it has also created ethical dilemmas about total confidentiality of the screening results on the part of the physician, who is legally bound to divulge the knowledge to insurance companies which are eager to know, and may at one point deny medical or life insurance to the inheritor of the gene. Laws are soon likely to be introduced in North American States to protect the afflicted individuals. Nevertheless, this screening is fundamental to future developments in medical science such as possible gene therapy to correct the faulty genes.

In a large majority of most cancers, cancer susceptibility genes are not inherited. They are usually unleashed as a result of injury to the gene pool by physical or chemical agents which are harmful to the genetic material (DNA). Physical agents include various forms of radiation such as ultraviolet rays or X-rays. For example, those with poorly pigmented skin (e.g. the white population) are more susceptible to the development of skin cancer and melanomas (tumours of the pigment cells of the skin) after frequent or prolonged exposure to the sun. Ultraviolet-blocking chemicals (in sun-blocking lotions) can provide some but not complete protection.

Chemical agents which can do damage to the DNA molecules are called genotoxic agents, most of which are also potent carcinogens or cancer-producing agents. They are quite numerous in nature, and some have been artificially made, for example, many of the pesticides (e.g. DDT) and herbicides. Cigarette smoke as well as smoked or barbecued meat or fish products contain many compounds which are potent carcinogens. They include benzenes (in the tar component of cigarette smoke), heterocyclic amines and polycyclic aromatic hydrocarbons (in smoked/barbecued meat or fish). This is why lung cancer, undeniably recognized as the most preventable disease since directly related to smoking, has risen to epidemic proportions in the Western male population during the last century. This incidence has now started to plateau or even decline in the Western men because of a decline in smoking in this population over the past one or two decades. Unfortunately the story is the opposite for Western women who, because of a rise in the smoking habit, are now catching up with or even surpassing Western men in developing lung cancer. The same sad story applies to the whole human population in the East (China, India), where smoking is on the rise (thanks to the clever efforts of the tobacco industry). Stomach cancer occurs at a high rate in Japan because of the habit of consuming smoked fish, whereas colon cancer is higher in the West, because of higher consumption of beef fat and barbecued meat. We shall discuss more about the relationship of diet to cancer at a later point.

As mentioned earlier, alteration of a single gene is usually inadequate to convert a normal cell into a cancer cell. Following the initial injury, the cells try to recover (or possibly repair the altered gene) by increased multiplication. Cancer scientists, who have studied the process of carcinogenesis, have arbitrarily named the initial event as 'initiation'. Eventual conversion of the 'initiated' cell into a cancer cell is believed to be dependent on one or more additional genetic alterations caused by the same or other carcinogenic agents branded as 'tumour promoters.' In essence, exposure to these agents causes further damage to the genetic material or the DNA. These agents may be certain chemical by-products within our body or extraneous agents introduced into the body from our environment.

Irrespective of the source of the carcinogen, whether exogenous (outside the body) or endogenous (inside the body), sequential alterations occur in the initiated cell leading to a full-fledged cancer. Some of the stages in this transition are recognizable under microscope by a pathologist, when cancer appears in a solid tissue (that is, tissues other than blood forming cells). These stages are given sequential names: *hyperplasia* (increased cell multiplication leading to a thickening of the tissue; this stage is reversible); *metaplasia* (abnormal appearance of a tissue at a wrong site; also a reversible stage in most cases); *neoplasia* (a benign tumour, which can be cured by surgical removal; this stage is not reversible and is often precancerous); *carcinoma in situ* (a locally invasive stage of cancer which has not spread elsewhere, and which may be curable by resection; this stage is not only irreversible but also very prone to development of the next stage, a highly invasive cancer); a full-fledged cancer (which has usually invaded normal tissues and often spread to distant sites, termed as *metastasis*; this is, of course, irreversible).

Once the cancer cells have reached an invasive stage, they start destroying normal cells and eventually enter blood or lymphatic vessels to reach other organs. However, the seeding of cells in a distant organ may not always lead to a new cancer in the new site. These cells may remain dormant for a long time before they start growing. Often their ability to grow at a distant site depends on the 'soil' or the new environment. If the environment is conducive to cancer cell multiplication or attraction of new blood vessels for nourishing the tumour (an event known as *angiogenesis*), then *metastasis* occurs quickly. A variety of protein molecules known as growth factors (which help cancer cell growth) and angiogenic factors (helping new blood vessel formation), produced by cancer cells or normal body cells in the cancer micro-environment, have been discovered and helped cancer scientists to design new therapies to block cancer cell multiplication or *angiogenesis*.

Diet (Nutrition) and Cancer

This is a major research area which has provided newer leads for prevention of certain cancers. As discussed earlier, diets such as smoked meat/fish or other foods known to contain carcinogenic chemicals should be avoided at all costs, and there is no controversy in this regard. A lot of controversy still remains as to 'what is a healthy diet which is perfect for health and at the same time least carcinogenic or even protective against cancer?' I wish to primarily emphasize those areas which have gained some scientific validity. There is no doubt that colon cancer in men is promoted by high meat (beef) and fat consumption, typical of the North American diet, until recently. This is why there has been a tremendous discrepancy in the incidence of colon cancer in the Japanese (low) versus the North American (high), which is not explained by genetic reasons. First generation Japanese immigrants to the North America who have adopted the food habits of the new country, have now caught up with the North Americans in contracting colon cancer. There is no doubt that a high fibre, low-fat diet reduces the risk of colon cancer. Relationship of a high-fat diet to the promotion of breast cancer in women, although not proven, remains a strong possibility.

Based on a variety of reasons, which cannot be discussed in this short article, one may comfortably suggest that an intelligent, commonsense approach to dietary habits can reduce cancer risk substantially. A diet consisting of low fat, high fibre (grains and vegetables), lean animal proteins (milk, fish, poultry) or vegetable proteins (a variety of grains, e.g. lentils, peas, and beans with a high protein content), and fresh fruits (citrus fruits contain vitamin C and flavonoids which are antioxidants, protecting DNA from damage by oxygen radicals; most fruits also contain high fibre and valuable minerals some of which are said to have protective effects) is not only good for reducing cancer risk, but also good for reducing the risk of heart disease and stroke. Vitamin A (natural, such as in milk), or its synthetic derivatives (such as Retinoic acid) and carotenoids (such as α and β carotenes) in the diet have also been shown to reduce the risk of numerous cancers.

There are certain claims, which remain to be validated by a larger body of scientific evidence, that certain food supplements or spices can protect against certain cancers. For example, consumption of tea (both black and green, as the typical drink) or spices such as fresh ginger, garlic and turmeric have been reported to reduce the risk of colon cancer. Onion is claimed to lower the risk of stomach cancer and soyabean products to reduce the risk of prostate cancer. Further scientific research is needed with these agents, in animals as well as humans. For example, topical application of some constituents of ginger, e.g. ginger oil or ginger extract, has proven to reduce the risk of skin cancer in mice, produced in the laboratory by painting of carcinogenic chemicals on the skin.

Our Immune System and Cancer

We are fortunate to possess a cell type (a class of lymphocytes, a lineage of white blood cells) known as the 'Natural Killer' (NK) cells which are produced in the bone marrow. When properly activated, these have the ability to recognize and kill cancer cells. This cell class was discovered only two decades ago and has only recently been exploited for treating certain types of cancer. Since cancer cells are genetically altered, they also express certain recognition markers on their cell surface which can be recognized by NK cells of the Immune System, so that in a healthy individual, a whole army of NK cells continuously polices our tissues against the development of cancer in order to nip it in the bud. Genetically deficient mice which lack in NK cells develop many more cancers in their lifetime.

If NK cells are fully competent in doing their job properly, then why do we succumb to cancer at all? Answers to this question have only been partly obtained in recent years. First, during the evolution of sequential genetic changes, some cancers, when first recognized, have also developed mechanisms to resist killing by NK cells. Fortunately, this is not a universal phenomenon. In a majority of cases, cancer cells develop mechanisms to disarm NK cells, so that NK cells remain inactive in the presence of the can-

cer. How does this happen? First, certain cancer cells themselves acquire the ability to make molecules that can
render NK cells ineffective. In other cases, cancer cells do
this indirectly by inducing certain white blood cells of the
host, known as macrophages, to make these NK cell disarming molecules. One of these NK cell disarming molecules has
been identified by our laboratory and subsequently by others as a simple small molecule known as prostaglandin E_2
(PGE_2).

We discovered that PGE_2 disarms NK cells by two
mechanisms. First, it shuts off the production in the body of
a key hormone-like growth factor known as interleukin–2,
which is essential for the functional activation or arming of
NK cells so that they are equipped with packages of killer
molecules needed to kill cancer cells. Interleukin–2
normally binds to its 'receptors' on the surface of NK cells
before the NK cells can be activated by this growth factor.
PGE_2, the NK disarming molecule, also shuts off the development of these receptors on the surface of NK cells. This is
the second mechanism by which PGE_2 inactivates NK cells.
Having gained the information of these mechanisms by
which NK cells are disarmed in the presence of a cancer, we
wondered whether we could exploit this knowledge to reac-
tivate NK cells in cancer-bearing animals.

A simple, logical approach was to block the production
of PGE_2 in the body with certain drugs. PGE_2 is a molecule
which is produced in abundance at the site of inflammation
such as in arthritic joints, causing pain. Doctors, for several
decades, have used a number of drugs of the aspirin family
such as aspirin, indomethacin and ibuprofen to block PGE_2
production and relieve arthritic inflammation and pain.

These drugs are reasonably effective. As aspirin often leads to other side effects in high doses, our laboratory chose treatment with indomethacin which can be given to cancer-bearing mice in their drinking water. Indomethacin therapy, when given early, was effective in reducing the growth of breast cancer in mice as well as preventing their metastasis (spread to distant sites). This therapy also rejuvenated NK cells in the cancer bearing host. However, when cancer was advanced, i.e. had already spread to distant organs, this therapy was ineffective.

We soon found the reasons. The body was still incompetent in producing enough interleukin–2 required for an adequate activation and multiplication of the army of NK cells so that they could effectively destroy cancer cells. The logical solution was to provide interleukin–2 in addition to indomethacin. Fortunately, a decade ago, manufacturing of interleukin–2 became possible with the help of bacteria by genetic engineering techniques, so that an adequate supply of bacteria-made interleukin–2 had been available. Cancer scientists at the National Cancer Institute, USA, had already started using this drug for cancer therapy. Injection of interleukin-2 produced responses in animals as well as in certain forms of human cancer. We found that the combination of indomethacin with interleukin–2 was far more effective than either drug given alone in experimental animals. This combination therapy succeeded in curing a variety of advanced cancers in mice as well as certain human cancers grown in immunodeficient mice. Our laboratory then applied this combination therapy to two types of advanced human cancers: kidney cancer and melanoma patients, resulting in very good responses. However, additional research is needed to improve this combination therapy further before it can be available as a routine treatment for selected types of cancer. This example is only a minute component of current research designed to deploy our immune system to fight cancer.

There are a variety of new approaches such as designing of cancer vaccines with genetic engineering, creation of 'magic bullets' by coupling cancer-killing drugs with cancer-recognizing antibodies, and gene-therapy to activate the immune system against cancer, etc. Doubtlessly, some of the new therapies will make their way to clinical practice within the next decade.

How do we keep our immune system in good functional order to fight cancer as well as infectious diseases? A healthy body and mind are both recognized as crucial to the health of our immune system including the functioning of NK cells. Thus, a healthy life-style including a healthy diet is a good basic approach. Sustained moderate physical activity, which keeps us generally fit, has also been proven to improve NK cell function. Interestingly, there is some evidence to indicate that mental relaxation, happiness, and stress-relieving exercises and meditation (to detach oneself from common day-to-day events which can produce stress) are also conducive to the function of the immune system, because of certain brain-derived hormones which indirectly help immune cell function.

Of the numerous hormones, melatonin has recently been claimed to be a key member. This hormone is produced by a minute gland in the brain known as the 'pineal body,' the level of the hormone rising during deep sleep as well as following deep meditation. This hormone has also influence on our sleep cycle. Unfortunately, however, out-landish claims of 'cure-all' properties of this hormone has led to an enormous misuse of this drug, which is available over the counter in USA but not in Canada. Claims have also been made that the drug can slow down the aging process. These claims have not been validated by rigorous scientific tests. It is highly likely that this 'over the counter' drug is not needed if we train ourselves to engage our body to produce enough melatonin.

Future Directions in Cancer Prevention and Cure

Many cancers, if properly localized and diagnosed early, are curable by modern surgery. Once the primary cancer has invaded normal tissues or spread to other sites, surgery alone is usually ineffective. Traditional therapies such as radiotherapy and chemotherapy, or combination therapies, can still cure certain forms of cancer or signifi-cantly improve the useful lifespan of the patient by causing a prolonged remission. For example, slightly more than half of childhood cancers can now be cured. In others, however, in spite of considerable progress in research, the mortality rate has not changed substantially. Newer modalities of combination therapies inclusive of hormones, anti-hormones, immunotherapy, vaccines, bone marrow trans-plantation, and gene therapy may hold strong promise in specific types of cancer. It should be emphasized that cancer is not a single disease, and thus cancer therapy has to be custom-designed for the individual cancer type.

Prevention and Chemo-intervention (to prevent a precancerous cell from becoming a cancerous cell) both remain as more important goals. Effective prevention relies to a large extent on extensive public education. Our research has revealed that immune cells such as NK cells are capable of recognizing an altered cell in the body at the precancerous stage. This fact raises the hope that intervention is possible by boosting the immune system in certain cases. Only future research will tell whether such hope is realistic. It is also possible that individuals who have inherited cancer susceptibility genes may benefit from gene therapy in the future, designed to correct these faulty genes in the appropriate tissue. It is unlikely that this will happen in the immediate future.

More research is also needed on natural compounds which may have anticancer activity. One example is the discovery of 'Taxol', a plant product which has proven to be of considerable benefit in certain cancers. There are many more waiting for their discovery, in particular, from indigenous plants in India, with proper scientific tools and testing. Great care must be taken by scientists to resist the temptation of making premature claims which have often hindered the progress of medical science.

11

Acupuncture

M. LONNIE WU

My Path to Profession

Chinese medicine always felt natural to me. I experienced the phenomenon of *Qi* (pronounced *chee*), which means prana or life force at an early age when I was asked to help massage a sore muscle or apply pressure to certain points on my father's back. I could feel the coursing of energy from within his body. I realized even then that I could receive energy from objects that I touched. I had a feeling, even then, that I could help people by sharing this energy.

I grew up with the smell of herbs, drying as they hung upside down or steaming in boiling pots. Our kitchen shelves were lined with jars containing all sorts of herbal mixtures. Herbal mixtures were not only intended for illness, but for fortification and celebration as well. Herbs would be specifically chosen for an aching back, menstrual cramps or to strengthen a mother after childbirth, insuring healthy milk for the baby.

In our home, dinner always began with a 'tang'—a soup of herbs which either addressed the season, general health or the specific condition of someone in the family. In this way, each leaf, root or bulb was recognized and honoured because it was giving its unique gift of nourishment to us. Each item on the table had a purpose: fish for the brain, roots for clear skin and greens for the eyes.

Despite this, the conflict between East and West existed even in our household. When I decided that I wanted to take up an apprenticeship in Chinese medicine, my father said that his medicine was old-fashioned, urging me to study Western medicine instead. Following the footsteps of my girl cousins, I entered a nursing programme. I was a member of one of first Code Blue Teams in New York and later worked in the first intensive care units there.

Nevertheless, I became more and more dissatisfied with the concept and practice of healing in allopathic (Western) medicine. It was clear to me that medical and surgical procedures did not necessarily relieve suffering, and all too often, the process of passing into the next life was a medical horror. The turning point came for me in the dramatic conjunction of two events. One day my son came home with a virulent case of chicken pox. He was crying miserably with itchy bumps and fever. I tried calamine lotion and everything else that friends suggested—all to no avail. My father offered to take care of him, and I went to my night shift at the hospital. That night, despite great effort, I lost a sixteen year old boy who had overdosed on methadone. In the morning, I dragged myself home with a heavy heart. As I opened the front door, I was greeted by a grinning boy whose fever was gone. My father had brewed a concoction causing the blisters to erupt more quickly, thereby relieving the discomfort and reducing the fever. The neighbourhood children, untreated or treated by Western medical methods, were all sick for a week to ten days longer than was my son.

Following this event, I began to study acupressure (a form of massage incorporating acupuncture meridians and points). Then in 1978, I suffered a serious back injury and was unable to work. After two months of physical therapy, I convinced my insurance company to pay for some acupuncture treatments. They allowed me one week of treatment. I received two treatments a day and was given herbs to drink. When I returned to my orthopedist, I was greatly improved and ready to return to work. He discounted the acupuncture treatments as placebo medicine! I realized then that I must honour my own concepts of health and return to my own cultural traditions.

Acupuncture is part of ancient, traditional Chinese medicine, having developed over a period of at least 3,000 years as one of several interrelated techniques. Archeological finds of the late Shang Dynasty (c. 1000 B.C.) reveal acupuncture needles as well as divination bones on which were inscribed notes on medical problems. Metal needles were introduced by 800 B.C. and gold needles were recently excavated from a tomb dated 300 B.C. As early as the Han Dynasty (206 B.C.–A.D. 220), the basics of Chinese medical theory were in place: the concepts of yin and yang, the five phases, channel theory, various needling methods and a pharmacopoeia. Chinese medicine continued to develop in later dynasties as the fundamental concepts were refined and expanded. The tradition we see today is a reflection of a constantly evolving art, and yet it is one that is only beginning to be recognized and appreciated in this country.

How Does Acupuncture Work?

In 1987, I was asked to write about how acupuncture works. In that article, I wrote: 'The acupuncture needle, when inserted into the body, acts like a lightning rod uniting the bioelectrical energies or Qi of the human body with that of the universe. . . . If there is a deficiency in the body, the needle placed in carefully chosen points will draw in energy. Likewise, if there is an excess in the body, the needle will either send the excess out of the body or redirect the excess to fill the deficient areas of the body.' Now, nearly a decade later, I realize that my statement expresses only a part of the truth. Today I would wish to place greater emphasis on the spiritual and emotional components of the tradition. Years of work with my patients has served to confirm my deep belief in the interconnectedness and interdependence of the human body with the mind and spirit as well as the external environment.

It has been suggested that the locations of the acupuncture points themselves were accidentally discovered when a person was struck in one part of the body only to find that a pain or disease elsewhere in the body was unexpectedly relieved. We now understand the cause of this phenomenon: there is a correlation in the flow of energy between various parts of the body. We call these flow-channels, meridians or pathways. It is believed that monks practising internal yoga breathing could feel the movement of Qi through their bodies and, in describing this and observing clinical trials and errors, energy pathways were mapped.

What, then, is this Qi? It can be described as prana or bioelectrical energy. For many, especially in the West, this may be to explain one mystery with another! Have you ever held your palms facing each other, close but not touching, and felt a fuzzy feeling or a pull growing between them? This is Qi—powerful, moving and unseen. Before birth, there is the divine or heavenly Qi that unites with our ancestral Qi (RNA/DNA) to create our life force. Later we are nourished by grains from the earth, combined with air Qi. These are transformed into vital energy (yang) and blood (yin). Blood is needed to make Qi, and it is Qi that moves the blood. One cannot exist without the other. If one is weakened, the other will be affected. We have many words that describe what happens when Qi is diseased. Qi is sometimes characterized as 'reckless'. In this condition, the blood will run out of control, resulting in hemorrhage. When Qi is 'stagnant,' energy will be blocked, causing pain or tumor formation. The first question asked in Chinese medicine is whether the problem at hand is primarily yin or yang—is it an imbalance in the Qi or an imbalance in the blood?

Fourteen Pathways

There are 14 main pathways or meridians, 12 of these are named after the organs through which they pass: the stomach, spleen, large intestine, etc. Apart from these meridians, there are many more connecting channels that allow the movement of energy throughout the body. The acupuncture points act like relay stations moving this bio-electrical energy or Qi through the channels. The result of needling depends upon the point stimulated as each has its own function.

As the location of points and therapeutic characteristics were recognized, they were given names. In the West, a numerical system is used to name the points. For instance, the kidney meridian consists of 27 points of entry enumerated in order: KI 1, KI 2, etc. For those who learn the Chinese names, however, there is a much clearer understanding of the use of these points. The point, Kidney 9 (*zhu bin*), for example, means 'house guest.' This is a point that I use often on pregnant women because, as the name suggests, it strengthens or builds the foetus—guest of its mother's womb. Some names suggest emotional, spiritual and mental implications of the points. For example, the Chinese name for the point Bladder 47 is *hun men* or spirit soul gate. This name refers to its governance over the *hun,* the spiritual soul which resides in the liver. *Hun* is associated with intuition, imagination and higher consciousness—the yang movement directed upward toward heaven. Bladder 42 or animal soul door (*po hu*) refers to the point governing the animal soul which resides in the lungs. *Po* is associated with passion, instinct and attachment.

Basic Concepts of Chinese Medicine

Chinese medicine is based upon the observation of nature. The Tao, the way of nature, is at the heart of

Chinese philosophy with the principle of yin and yang at the root of this belief. In the symbol of Tao, we see that black and white aspects are in perfect balance. The yang represents the masculine aspects: positive, expansion, fire; the yin represents the feminine: negative, contraction, water. Where yin becomes thinner, yang is stronger. If you look further, you will see there is a white circle in the yang and a black circle in the yin, thus signifying the duality of nature that exists in all forms. Within yin, there is yang. Within yang, there is yin. This is the ever changing phenomenon of all living beings. The Chinese do not believe in absolutes or ideals: everything is relative, flexible, and ever changing.

Cold is seen as yin in nature, but at the extreme of cold, there is heat—as in dry ice which can burn. Conversely, a fever, which is yang, can cause shivering. This is the balance that the body naturally tries to achieve from moment to moment without our effort or awareness. But in illness, this harmony is disrupted. In Chinese medicine, we try to re-establish balance through lifestyle changes, diet, herbs, and acupuncture.

The ancients believed that what nature is composed of, we are composed of. Each human being is a microcosmic part of the macrocosm. We have within us the five elements or phases: earth, metal, water, wood, and fire. Each of these elements has a personality and an internal milieu connected with who we are. No aspect of the person functions as an independent, discrete entity. Each physical function is connected to an emotional aspect. Each governs an organ, sensory perception or season. There is an interplay between them that keeps our physical and emotional relationship in balance.

Seasons and Archetypes

In Chinese Medicine, we prepare ourselves for the changes of the season by honouring and observing what we eat and how we dress. The body's inner dynamics are affected by the climatic factors such as wind, cold, fire, dryness, dampness, and summer heat. These are the six evils or pernicious influences that can penetrate the body and cause illness if the body is already weakened by an imbalance of yin and yang. For example, a person living in Southern California is sometimes exposed to desert-like conditions characterized by heat, dryness and wind. Some individuals are quick to anger and prone to irritation and agitation during windy conditions. According to the *Nei Ching,* The Yellow Emperor's Classic text: 'The Wind circulates within the Liver.' I encourage patients with liver disharmonies to try to stay out of the wind and to wear clothing that covers their bodies, especially the neck where the wind can penetrate 'the wind gate.' Since the liver controls the emotions, taking care of it will also take care of how we act and react during stress.

One can find out which archetype most describes us by looking at the descriptions shown in the five element chart illustrated on the facing page. As you can see, the liver, which is the wood element, also controls tendons and ligaments. Therefore, the liver is like a tree or plant. When the wind blows, the branches will sway or the leaves will shake. When a Wood person has been affected by too much

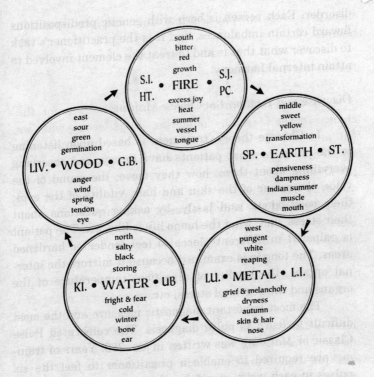

FIRE
south
bitter
red
growth
S.I. HT. • • S.J. PC.
excess joy
heat
summer
vessel
tongue

WOOD
east
sour
green
germination
LIV. • • G.B.
anger
wind
spring
tendon
eye

EARTH
middle
sweet
yellow
transformation
SP. • • ST.
pensiveness
dampness
indian summer
muscle
mouth

WATER
north
salty
black
storing
KI. • • UB
fright & fear
cold
winter
bone
ear

METAL
west
pungent
white
reaping
LU. • • L.I.
grief & melancholy
dryness
autumn
skin & hair
nose

internal wind, spasms can occur. This is diagnosed by
expensive tests in Western medicine as twitches, cramps,
epilepsy, trigeminal neuralgia or strokes, etc. In Traditional
medicine, by contrast, all these symptoms are simply
referred to as a Wind disorder. By feeling the pulse, we find
a tight, wiry quality. We examine the patient and direct the
treatments towards discharging the wind and strengthen-
ing the liver. By simply treating the liver, we can also clear
up other problems along that meridian, such as an eye

disorder. Each person is born with genetic predispositions
toward certain imbalances, and it is the practitioner's task
to discover what that is and to treat the element involved to
attain internal harmony.

Diagnosis and Treatment in Chinese Medicine

In Chinese theory, treatment is based upon listening
to the pulse, to what patients have to say, and observing
everything about them: how they move; the sound of the
voice; the colour of the skin and hair; vitality of the eyes;
their body odour, and lastly, by asking questions about
their stress, diet, what the home life is like, etc. The patient
is palpated in different places to feel tender or hardened
areas. The tongue is examined because it mirrors the internal organs, the quality of digestion, temperature of the
organs and the degree of stress, etc.

The most important diagnostic measure and the most
difficult to learn is pulse diagnosis. The celebrated Pulse
Classic or *Mai Jing* was written in A.D. 280. Years of training are required to enable a practitioner to feel the six
pulses in each wrist, signifying the condition of the twelve
major organs, the six emotions, the climate within the body,
and its humors. Diagnosis is based upon the twenty-eight
pulse qualities. This is the moment of sacred listening and
sharing between the patient and the practitioner. In China,
when a patient feels the need for medical treatment, he
does not say that he's going to the doctor, but rather says,
' I'm going to have my pulses read.'

Listening to the pulses is *the* essential diagnostic technique. Next in importance is listening to the patient himself

or herself. Not one bit of information is discounted. I write everything down and eventually all these pieces fit into a giant puzzle that identifies that individual as a whole being. It is only then that I formulate a plan of action. Will it be only herbal, only acupuncture, or both? Perhaps I will suggest meditation or dietary adjustment. Perhaps massage and stress relaxation techniques are needed. I have often written down a list of ten or more initial problems or conditions, but by narrowing this down to one picture, I have found that the treatment itself is quite simple. I find that the most difficult aspect of my work is treating patients who have already tried every avenue of conventional medicine. Their condition, often complicated by drugs and surgery, has become quite chronic. We may not be able to relieve every symptom, but there is generally some relief over a period of time as we keep filling in the empty meridians with Qi. In situations like cancer, acupuncture can relieve the symptoms of pain and nausea from chemotherapy. Over and over again, I have seen AIDS patients feeling better, having stronger immune systems and living longer than anticipated with Western medicine.

I consider dietary change as one of the most important aspects of my treatment programme. I ask all my patients to submit a diet journal so I can see how food is used and how diet may be influencing the disharmony. The word for nutrition in Chinese is made from the words for construction and nourishment. In Chinese medicine, we do not look at food as calories, fats, vitamin content, etc., but rather which organ might be affected: is it a cold or hot energy food? Does it affect the upper body or lower body, and what taste is it—sweet, sour, salty, pungent or bitter?

Herbal treatment also is quite different from Western medicine in the way six patients with herpes, for example, might be treated. In the West, all would most likely be given the same medication. In Chinese medicine, these patients are treated as individuals with six different patterns of disharmony. Each will be given a prescription based upon those differences. In allopathic medicine, an antibiotic is designed to cover a wide range of infection no matter where it is located in the body. In Chinese herbal theory, the patient's inherent weakness is noted and herbs are given to strengthen the diseased system along with herbs to treat the specific problem. Herbs are directed to where the action should take place, which could be the head, nose, shoulders—whatever part is in need. The word 'cold' is *shang feng,* which means 'injured by the wind.' We see this penetration past the body's immune defences by the external wind as an invasion of an external evil force. The practitioner must also decide if this is a cold wind or a hot wind. The person with 'wind cold' would have a runny, red nose, sneezing and feel chilled. The patient with 'wind heat' would be feverish and have a sore throat. This difference between heat and cold requires different herbs. Even a cold is not a straight forward diagnosis in Chinese medicine!

Sometimes it is difficult to know which came first: an emotional trauma or a physical illness. For example, a young child suffers from chronic colds and upper respiratory problems. He cannot take deep breaths and sighs often. We ask: 'Did this child simply catch a cold which weakened his lungs or did he experience inconsolable grief through the death of his dog, thus weakening his lungs?' As shown in the chart, the emotion of the lung is grief.

The Goal of Health and Healing

Chinese medicine is like peeling the layers of an onion. Time must be given for the psyche to allow the next layer to be revealed to the practitioner and to the patient himself. There is great joy in seeing a patient discover truth about himself or herself and find new tools for healing. In so many cases, it is not what lies on the surface that counts but what is below. A back problem may reflect years of stored emotional issues that need to be accessed before the back can truly heal. A gentleman I treated many years ago came with a nagging neck problem. Around the third treatment, I told him that his neck was problematic, but that the underlying reason was grief. He smiled and indicated, in various ways, that he was wealthy and important—he had nothing to grieve about. One morning, several treatments later, he called and said, 'What did you do to me? Soon after I left your office, I had to pull over to the side of the road. I cried and sobbed like I haven't done since I was a little boy. But you know what? That neck pain is almost gone!'

During my treatments, I may give the patient visualizations, guided imageries, or meditations to do while they are lying with their needles in place. I believe healing takes place when the body is at rest, free from stress or mental activity. Most often, the patient will fall into a relaxed sleep and awaken reporting that they had the deepest rest. Many report that they never fall asleep anywhere but in their own beds but, to their amazement, have fallen asleep during their treatments—despite the needles.

The following was written by one of my patients: 'Acupuncture has shown me that rather than covering over what needs to be released inside me, I need to let what is already there come to the surface. Having acupuncture is like working outward from my soul clearing the debris blocking a stream's flow. . . . I can hear my cells dancing with joy and relief.'

In a capitalistic society such as ours, it is not surprising that the billion dollar alternative medicine industry is at last attracting the attention of mainstream medicine, supported by such groups as the National Institute of Health. Consumers are dissatisfied with costly treatments that don't work. I see these two medicines, not as competitive but complementary, and I see how they can work together almost daily. Both exist for the benefit of humankind. Consumers must work to influence public policy and ensure that they have choices in their care. To do otherwise is to lose freedom, dignity and fullest health.

12

Yoga and Holistic Health

Y oga is skill in action,' states the Bhagavad Gita, the quintessence of the Upanishads and a comprehensive text on Yoga. But this is not intended to mean action in just the narrow sense of physical movement. For, besides exercises for improving the 'skill' of our body, yoga also comprises techniques that transform our intellect, mind and emotions, and provides a complete philosophy for living. Yoga is a way of life. It is a science of holistic living.

In order to live holistically, we must develop 'skill' in all aspects of our life. Sri Aurobindo regarded yoga as a methodical effort toward self-perfection through developing our latent potential at the physical, vital, mental, intellectual, and spiritual levels. And the most fundamental step

we can take toward expanding the limits of our consciousness is to gain mastery over our mind.

This is also the key to good health and happiness in
today's world. Great advances in medical science over the
past century have reduced the incidence of most of the
physical diseases that have plagued humanity for centuries.
Ever better drugs and surgical techniques have led to the
eradication of most infectious diseases and the control of
many metabolic disorders. Soon even routine genetic inter-
ventions may be possible. But these techniques are less
than effective against the new and ever more common
causes of ill health—chronic stress and psychosomatic ailments.

Conventional medicine, by concentrating on a physical
and mechanistic approach to healing, can do little to relieve
conditions such as these, since they are caused more by life-
style and attitudes than by physiological anomalies. The
frenetic pace of modern life exposes many people to continuous, unrelieved stress. And if we are largely sedentary in
our habits and overindulge in health damaging substances
and foods, our well-being and fitness will be further compromised. Eventually stress may manifest itself in the form of
physical disease or mental breakdown. Modern medicine
has countered with symptom-suppressing treatments,
which do little to tackle the root cause of the problem. As a
result, health has come to be regarded as a static state in
which disease is absent, rather than as a dynamic growth
process in which we feel truly well on both the physical and
mental levels. But there is no reason to settle for anything
less than a positive sense of well-being.

Yoga has a lot to offer as we approach the 21st century. It gives us the means to complement medical technology with a holistic system of healthcare that addresses the problems of the mind and spirit, as well as those of the body. Patanjali, who wrote the classic text on yoga nearly 3000 years ago, described it as 'a science of the mind.' And it is through teaching us to control our mind, our desires, and our reactions to stress, that yoga can fundamentally help us.

Mastery of the mind involves two aspects: the ability to concentrate our attention on any given subject or object, and the capacity to quieten our mind at will. Though most people have developed the first aspect to some degree, very few of us can lapse into inner peace even accidentally, let alone at will. Yoga is an intelligent, skilful means for making the mind quiet, rather than a brutal, mechanical technique for stopping it.

All aspects of yoga work toward this in some way, thus bringing us closer to our goal. Yoga develops our ability to maintain inner peace at all times, in all our actions, and thereby achieve physical and mental health. This calmness in action is the secret to attaining the 'skill' referred to in the Bhagavad Gita.

Health and Yoga Therapy

According to the World Health Organisation (WHO) the state of health is defined as a state of complete physical, mental and social well-being and not merely an absence of disease or infirmity. WHO also suggests a fourth dimension—spiritual well-being. It is clear from this definition that health and ill-health are not two discrete entities as commonly understood but health should be conceived as a continuous function indicating the state of well-being.

The approach of yoga therapy is based on the holistic concept of human beings: the five 'sheaths' to existence, of which the physical frame is only the first. The second is the vital body that is made up of *prāṇa,* the life energy that flows through us in invisible channels known as *nāḍis.* The third is the mind (our emotions and thoughts), the fourth is the higher intellect (perfect thought and knowledge), and the final sheath is the 'abode of bliss.' The bliss sheath is thought to consist of the positive energy that is associated with the divine. It is from this sheath that the inner peace essential to true happiness emanates.

Disease is seen to arise through imbalance in any of the three lower sheaths of existence. In the physical, prāṇic, and mind sheaths, ego consciousness, which is centred around the self, predominates and so harmony in these sheaths can be easily disturbed. The fourth and fifth sheaths are permeated by a wider, universal consciousness and cannot be perturbed. When we are truly healthy, the positive energy in the highest sheath percolates freely through the lower ones and brings total harmony and balance to all our faculties. But though the harmony of the higher sheaths is constant, the free movement of bliss can be blocked by imbalances in the lower sheaths.

According to *Yoga Vāsiṣṭha,* a great text on yoga, there are two types of physical illness, and each requires a different approach. The first are the illnesses with a strong physical element, such as contagious diseases and accidental injuries. These are most effectively dealt with by conventional medicine, though yoga can play a substantial supporting role. Yoga also helps prevent the occurrence of such ailments by improving our general health and making us less accident-prone.

The other type of illness arises through disturbances in the mind sheath and includes all the psychosomatic and degenerative ailments. In these disorders, psychological factors play a much greater role, and conventional treatment alone is not usually an effective cure. According to Indian beliefs, such ailments are thought to be caused by mental diseases called *ādhis*. These arise when excessively strong feelings of like or dislike become amplified and established, acting to distort personality and to obstruct the flow of positive energy to the lower sheaths. This causes imbalances that result in physical ailments and also make us feel restless and discontented.

The inner peace that is our natural state is generated by the positive energy from the bliss-sheath. When the flow of this energy is interrupted by *ādhis*, our sense of wellbeing is diminished and, in our attempt to regain it, we may be further aggravating the problem by behaving inappropriately. We may, for example, find ourselves eating the wrong foods, living in unhealthy surroundings, lapsing into negative states of mind, or driving ourselves too hard. But these methods give only temporary relief and may, in fact, be damaging our health.

With psychosomatic ailments, yoga provides the vital element that modern therapies lack and acts directly on the mental imbalances that underlie them. While *emotion-culturing* and *meditation* make us aware of the tyranny of thoughts and emotions, *happiness-analysis* teaches us how to look within ourselves to find peace and satisfaction. At the same time, other yoga practices facilitate the restoration of health at other levels as well. This effectively complements medical techniques which improve the situation physically but are unable to eradicate the primary cause of the problem.

Happiness Analysis for Lifestyle Change

This involves trying to understand the nature of bliss, the inner peace that characterizes the fifth level of being. It basically embodies the realization that happiness comes from within and is not dependent on material possessions or physical enjoyment.

Happiness is often associated with jubilation and excitement, or the satisfaction of achieving desires. But these sources of pleasure are temporary and are often followed by negative feelings such as tiredness or disillusionment. Real, sustainable inner peace involves no effort and engenders no fatigue. The texts of yoga describe complete happiness as a state of silence, where we are no longer troubled by unnecessary thoughts and fears, a state of perfect poise and freedom of choice.

Yogic practices lay the foundation needed for us to achieve this, but we must also try to identify consciously what perfect happiness is—and attempt to cultivate and maintain such a state for as long as we can. We should start by analysing our feeling of pleasure. Yogis claim that actions bring pleasure when they briefly evoke the inner silence that defines true happiness. When we obtain something we desire or attain a hard-won goal, at the very instance of success our thoughts vanish and our mind dips momentarily into the sheath of bliss. This is the source of pleasure as it tends to open up temporary channels to the higher sheath, hence evoking positive sensations. But this feeling is temporary and can tempt us to overindulge in the activity or substance that generated it.

If we can isolate and remember that brief moment of satisfaction, however, we can learn to generate it from within and free ourselves from dependency on external aids. At first we may not be able to maintain inner peace for long, but gradually we will become less vulnerable to negative influences. The likes and dislikes that can lead to *ādhis* will become less important and our growing awareness of universal consciousness will give meaning and coherence to every aspect of our life.

The Basis of Yoga Therapy

Yoga is fundamentally different from conventional medical practice in its approach to healthcare. Instead of trying to reduce the cause of disease to a single factor and to correct it using a specific cure, yoga aims to treat illness by improving health on all levels simultaneously and by restoring inner harmony.

Ill-health occurs when the total balance of perfect health is disturbed. And although the original disrupting influence may only affect one level at first, the disturbance soon spreads. All the five sheaths of existence interact, thus something that primarily affects the mind, say, can soon spread to the body and pranic sheaths. A bad day at work may make us irritable, for example, and it also increases stress reactions, makes our muscles tense, and often depletes our energy level, leading to chronic fatigue.

For this reason, yoga contains elements that address problems at every level—*āsanas* that relax and tone our muscles and massage our internal organs, *prāṇāyāma* that slows our breathing and regulates the flow of *prāṇa*, relaxation and meditation that act to calm our mind, and *emotion-culturing* produces equanimity. For just as negative influences spread disruption, positive action has repercussions as well. The different types of yoga practice augment each other and are more effective when done together. When we do the *āsanas* and stretch our muscles, muscular tension is released and we are able to relax easily. Likewise, when we relax the mind and release suppressed emotions, we tend to become less tense on physical level. Every element of yoga brings benefits throughout and also acts to amplify the effect of the other types of practices.

This is the essence of yoga therapy, both as a preventive and as a curative. Daily practice of a complete yoga session can restore our natural balance and harmony, bringing positive good health to all parts of our life—physical, mental, and spiritual.

The Therapeutic Potential of Yoga

Yoga is an ancient Indian science and way of life. In recent years the practice of yoga has become popular because it promotes positive health and is also useful in the prevention and treatment of diseases. The therapeutic potential of yoga has largely been investigated for stress-

related psychosomatic ailments. But with the recent interest in 'psycho-neuro-immunology' (the effect of the psyche
on the immune system), there is also a possibility that yoga
therapy can modify the course of infectious diseases.

One of the stress conditions which can definitely be
controlled through yoga practice is bronchial asthma.
Beneficial effects of specific yoga practices, such as
prāṇāyāmas,[1] or *kriyās,*[2] and an integrated approach of
yoga therapy (IAYT)[3] have been described. The IAYT acts at
different levels, viz physical, mental, emotional and spiritual, to correct imbalances, so that the asthma patient
requires less (or no) medicine while symptoms reduce significantly.

Patients with type II diabetes mellitus were also
shown to improve following yoga practice.[4] More recently
attempts have been made to understand these therapeutic
benefits in terms of changes at the cellular level.[5] Controlled studies on the benefits of yoga therapy for essential
hypertension have shown that yoga therapy compares fa-
vourably with biofeedback.[6] A study conducted in the UK on
patients with rheumatoid arthrities demonstrated that
yoga practice reduced symptoms and need for medicine,
while functions improved.[7]

Apart from the above-mentioned applications of yoga
as therapy in psychosomatic ailments, it is now known that
if patients with pathological anxiety practise specific yoga
techniques such as *prāṇāyāmas,* they show significant
improvement.[8] Schizophrenic patients are less easy to manage. However preliminary results show that there is a
period of six to eight weeks, during which the outcome is
questionable. If a programme of yoga is continued along

with psychotherapy and support, there is an objective and subjective improvement.[9]

Yoga practice has also been used in the rehabilitation of the mentally handicapped.[10] Nine months of yoga practice significantly improved the IQ, social adaptation and eye-hand coordination of 45 children with varying degrees of mental retardation, compared to a matched, non-yoga group. Yoga practice was also significantly more efficient than games in improving the physiological status of children at a remand home,[11] suggesting a role for yoga in the rehabilitation of institutionalized children.

The concept of psycho-neuro-immunology has given rise to interest in the idea that the practice of yoga can be used for the management of infectious diseases, such as pulmonary tuberculosis. A recent study[12] showed that two months of yoga therapy along with conventional, short term chemotherapy, caused conversion to negativity in a significantly shorter time, i.e. two weeks. This remarkably beneficial effect of yoga on the immune system has resulted in an interest in the effect of yoga therapy in cancer, and even in AIDS patients. It has been shown[13] that the practice of yoga reduces the unpleasant side-effects of chemotherapy in patients with cancer of the uterine cervix. It is also interesting to study scientifically investigated reports on cancer regression following meditation.[14] It is encouraging to note that there has been a scientific study which showed that AIDS patients benefited (clinically, psychologically, immunologically) from yoga therapy.[15] However more controlled studies are required to draw conclusions.

The objective of Vivekananda Kendra Yoga Research Foundation, or in short VK YOGAS, is to make yoga a socially relevant science by using modern scientific research to establish the usefulness of yoga in all walks of life. Over the last 15 years, the Yoga Therapy Research has drawn attention to the immense potentialities of yoga in health management. The published research papers in national and international journals appended in the end clearly show that we are heading for a major role in the use of the Integrated Approach of Yoga Therapy (IAYT) for prevention, treatment, long term rehabilitation and promotion of positive health.

REFERENCES

1. K. J. R. Murthy, B. K. Sahay, A. P. Seetharamaraju, R. Yogi, S. Madhavi, M. Venkatareddy, N. Annapoorna, M. Ramesh, P. Vijayalakshmi, & E. Reddy, (1984). "Effect of Pranayama (Rechaka-Puraka-Kumbhaka) on Bronchial Asthma: An Open Study." *Lung India* 2: 187–91.

2. Singh, V. (1987). "Kunjal: A Non-specific Protective Factor in Management of Bronchial Asthma." *Journal of Asthma* 24: 183–87.

3. Nagarathna, R. & Nagendra, H. R. (1985). "Yoga for Bronchial Asthma: A Controlled Study." *British Medical Journal* 291: 1077–79.

   Nagendra, H. R. & Nagarathna, R. (1986). "An Integrated Approach of Yoga Therapy for Bronchial Asthma: A 3–54 Month Prospective Study." *Journal of Asthma* 23(3): 123–37.

4. B. K. Sahay, B. Sadashivudu, R. Yogi, C. Bhaskaracharyulu, P. S. Raju, S. Madhavi, M. Venkatareddy, N. Annapoorna, & K. J. R. Murthy, (1982). "Biochemical Parameters in Normal Volunteers Before and After Yogic Practices." *Indian Journal of Medical Research* 76: 144–148.

5. Jain, S. C. & Talukdar, B. (1994). "Plasma and Eerythrocyte Lipid Peroxidation in Hypercholester-olemic Diabetic Subjects: Effect of Yoga Training." Paper presented at the 2nd National Conference on Yoga Therapy: Diabetes, Hypertension, Cardiovascular Diseases, organized by the Central Research Institute for Yoga, New.Delhi, February 3–5.

6. Patel, C. H. (1975). "Twelve Month Follow-up of Yoga and Bio-feedback in the Management of Hypertension." *Lancet* 1: 62–64.

7. I. Hanslock, R. Monro, R. Nagarathna, H. R. Nagendra, & N. V. Raghuram, (1994). "Measuring the Effects of Yoga in Rheumatoid Arthritis (A Letter)." *British Journal of Rheumatology* 33(8): 787–88.

8. Crisan, H. (1984). "Pranayama in Anxiety Neurosis—A Pilot Study." University of Heidelberg, MD thesis.

9. P. Raghuraj, R. Nagarathna, A. Saraswathi, H. Nunn, & S. Telles, (1995). "Effect of Yyoga on Schizophrenics." Paper presented at Richmond Fellowship Asia Pacific Forum International Symposium on "Innovations in Psychiatric Rehabilitation," November 23–25.

10. K. Uma, H. R. Nagendra, R. Nagarathna, S. Vaidehi, & R. Seetha-lakshmi, (1989). "The Integrated Approach of Yoga: A Therapeutic Tool for Mentally Retarded Children: A One Year Controlled Study." *Journal of Mental Deficiency Research* 33: 415–21.

11. S. Telles, S. Narendran, P. Raghuraj, R. Nagarathna, & H. R. Nagendra, (1977). "Comparison of Changes in Autonomic and Respiratory Parameters of Girls After Yoga and Games at a Community Home." *Perceptual and Motor Skills* 84: 251–57.

12. N. K. Manjunath, K. V. Naveen, R. Nagarathna, & S. Telles, (1996). "Yoga Therapy for Tuberculosis—An Application of Psycho-neuro-immunology." Paper presented at 17th Annual Conference of Indian Association of Biomedical Scientists, October 5–6.

13. Kannan, V. & Anantha, N. (1995). "Radiation Therapy and Yoga in the Treatment of Cancer of the Uterine Cervix." Paper presented at the Third International Conference on Frontiers in Yoga Research and Applications, organized by VK YOGAS, Bangalore, December 23–27.

14. Meares, A. (1982). "Stress, Meditation and the Regression of Cancer. *Practitioner* 226: 1607–9.

15. P. C. Madan, (1996). "To Study the Efficacy of Vibrionic Therapy and Transcendental Meditation in Management of HIV-positive Service Personnel." Paper presented at the First International Conference on Yoga in Daily Life, organized by VK YOGAS, Bangalore & ASK, Delhi, December 20–22.

13
Well-being and Spirituality

CHRIS LOVATO

All of us, in one way or another, are searching for a sense of satisfaction and contentment in life; the sense of feeling at peace with our world. At one time or another we have all experienced deep feelings of contentment, even if they are only momentary. We believe that there really is such a thing as well-being and we crave to live in that state all the time. This is our human quest. It is natural to seek happiness and we invest the whole of our energy in seeking it, despite its apparent elusiveness.

There are many ways to find satisfaction in this world. We spend our lives searching for a sense of well-being in such things as money, recognition, power, and physical pleasure. The problem is that we cannot depend on these worldly sources of satisfaction because each of them is only temporarily satisfying and soon we either tire of them or the world around us changes, telling us of something even better. If we examine our own lives, we find our search to be an endless roller coaster of ups and downs, happiness and sadness, elation and depression. This experience seems to be a natural part of the human condition. In an often-quoted passage from *The Prophet,* Kahlil Gibran reminds us:

> Some of you say, 'Joy is greater than sorrow,' and others say, 'Nay, sorrow is the greater.'
>
> But I say unto you, they are inseparable.
>
> Together they come, and when one sits alone with you on your board, remember that the other is asleep upon your bed.[1]

Can this vicious cycle be stopped? Where can we find a more stable source of well-being? How can we gain our freedom from a dependency on things that are forever changing and out of our control?

Ironically, modern culture tells us to look for happiness in the outer world, yet it is the outer world that distracts us from a more permanent and stable sense of well-being. Real happiness can only be attained through freedom *from* the outer world. It is within.

My Personal Journey

Many years ago, I journeyed to India in search of peace and happiness. As a young and single woman I had been lonely and longed for a companion. My job, material possessions, and friends could not satisfy the hunger I felt for inner joy and peace. My search for happiness led me on a spiritual quest to the holy city of Nasik where I spent my days with a Sadhu who was highly revered and loved by many as a spiritual father.

As a Westerner I found the living conditions in India to be very different from those to which I was accustomed. One evening, after many days of Satsang with the Nasik Sadhu, I realized all at once how utterly happy and contented I felt. I had all the feelings of joy and love I had longed for. How was this possible? My stomach hurt, I was constantly hungry, and my body ached more than I had ever experienced. Yet, my whole being vibrated with a joy I had never experienced. That moment was a great gift, as I suddenly and profoundly realized that the joy I had been waiting to receive from another human being was within my own self. It was a simple experience of the well-being that can be ours, regardless of external conditions.

Scott Peck opens his best-seller, *The Road Less Travelled,* with the simple yet bold observation that 'Life is difficult.'[2] If we examine our behaviour and attitudes, it becomes painfully obvious that his declaration is true despite our deepest desire that it be different. We try desperately to avoid this truth by searching unceasingly for perfect happiness in our relationships, in our jobs, social recognition, and in the things we can purchase with money. It is these very things that get us caught up in an endless cycle of emotional ups and downs.

Freedom through Meditation

Swami Turiyananda writes about meditation as a source of freedom from the world-based emotions that hold us in bondage:

Happiness and misery alternate in this world. Have you ever
seen anyone completely free from them? It is impossible: this
world is made up of pairs of opposites. By meditating on the
Atman one can get rid of them. This does not mean that there
will be no happiness or misery, but by God's grace they won't
be able to perturb one.[3]

Thus, meditation is essential in overcoming the un-
dependable nature of what the world offers and developing
a more consistent and enduring sense of well-being.

My own experience in practising meditation has been
that it has enhanced my sense of control and increased my
enjoyment of day-to-day living. More importantly, I see myself slowly developing a sense of inner strength and peace
that is stable. I am beginning to discover a place within
myself that is ever present, comforting, and renewing, despite the circumstances and continual ups and downs in my
daily life.

Meditation can be a bridge between Eastern and
Western paths to well-being. It has an ancient scientific
history as being the central means to well-being in the East
and a more recent history of documented scientific study in
the West. The current difference is that in Western science
it is viewed primarily as a means to physical and mental
well-being that has physically observable results. Eastern
thought begins at a deeper, more subtle level of satisfaction. From this perspective the object of meditation is
rooted in the spiritual plane. The results cannot be detected
by the tools of a science based on physical observations.
Indeed, we use the term 'spiritual' because the very thing
we are describing is metaphysical rather than physical in
its manifestation.

Clearly, we can find temporary pleasure in the things of the world. However, a stable sense of well-being can only be found within. Meditation is a practice that can lead to an inner sense of peace and tranquillity, it costs nothing, it is portable and it is available under all conditions. The effects of meditation on well-being have been described by Swami Lokeswarananda in *Practical Spirituality:* 'If you practise meditation regularly and in a correct manner, you become your own master and cease to be the slave of circumstances that you are now.'[4]

Conclusion

Once we accept the great truth that 'life is difficult' and that we cannot find our happiness in the things of this world, we can transcend this predicament. The search for well-being is our human right. The secret is that the well-being we seek lies deep within our selves. The key is to move away from external sources of happiness and toward the internal source of well-being that lies awaiting. The nature of this quest is spiritual as opposed to physical and it is a journey we must ultimately make alone.

REFERENCES

1. Gibran, Kahlil, *The Prophet,* 127th reprint (New York: Alfred A Knopf, Inc., 1995). First published in 1923.
2. Peck, M. Scott, *The Road Less Travelled* (New York: Simon and Schuster, 1978).
3. Swami Chetanananda, *Spiritual Treasures: Letters of Swami Turiyananda* (St. Louis, MO: Vedanta Society of St. Louis, 1992), 81.
4. Swami Lokeswarananda, *Practical Spirituality* (Calcutta: Ramakrishna Mission Institute of Culture).

14
Tribal Healthcare System

H. SUDARSHAN

Tribal people in India constitute 8% (70 million) of the total population of India. Even today some of the tribal communities have retained their traditional culture and indigenous knowledge. They have survived for more than 3000 years in various parts of India with their indigenous knowledge of health.

They have a holistic outlook on life and their indigenous knowledge is also holistic in nature. Till recently Mother Nature was the single largest factor influencing tribal culture. The tranquillity of tribal life was undisturbed by modernization. The tribals had their own self-sufficient economy closely linked to the simplicity of their life-styles and to their minimal requirements. All their needs were met by the abundance of virgin forests. Their life-style integrated well with the ecological cycle of the forests so that the sub-ecosphere of tribals never harmed or checked the growth of the larger ecosphere of the forest.

With my education in Western medicine I had initially thought that tribal people with whom I worked were totally 'ignorant' and they had to be taught 'modern' ideas of health. After living with tribal community for 16 years, I have learnt more from the wisdom of these people than I have taught them. Humility and willingness to study and learn the traditional knowledge system are the most important lessons I have learnt.

Problems of Modern Health Care System

The modern healthcare system in India inherited from the colonial rulers has inherent defects. Even after 50 years of independence we are unable to provide Primary Healthcare to all our people. In this regard, the following facts are to be noted.

1. Even now 50% of our primary health centres do not have a functional microscope to diagnose tuberculosis, malaria and leprosy.

2. Though we have 60,000 formulations available in the market, there is always a shortage of the most essential drugs needed for the treatment of major health problems like tuberculosis and malaria. Most of these drugs are either irrational, bannable or banned drugs. Quite a few drugs which are banned in Europe and U.S.A. are still being sold in this country. For the pharmaceutical companies,

profit seems to be more important than the health of the people.

3. Trained Allopathy doctors are unwilling to work in rural and tribal areas

Tribal Healthcare System

Tribal Medicine should really be called 'Tribal Health-care System' as it has more holistic approach to health than merely treating with herbal medicines. The tribals treat the body, mind and soul. They combine herbal medicine with prayers, sacrifices and good healthcare practices. Sick individuals are not left to themselves, the village community as a whole takes the responsibility of caring for them.

The life-styles and the relationship with forests play an important role in tribal healthcare system. The tribal people who live in the core area of reserved forests with access to forest resources have much better health status than the tribal people who are alienated from forests. The former do not suffer from appendicitis, colonic cancers, STD's, vitamin deficiencies, ischaemic heart diseases, hypertension, and other stress-induced illnesses.

The traditional knowledge of the various health practices and herbal medicines of Soliga tribal people are being documented by Vivekananda Girijana Kalyana Kendra (VGKK), B. R. Hills, Mysore district.

a) Traditional Health Practices

Conducting deliveries in squatting posture is a traditional practice and even now almost all the deliveries are conducted in squatting posture with the help of traditional birth attendants. The gravity and the better contraction of pelvic muscles in this posture help the mother to deliver the baby easily. The modern obstetric table seems to be more convenient for the doctor and nurse than to the mother! The Soliga mothers have very few obstetric complications because of this posture and several good 'Mother and Child Health' practices. The traditional birth attendants (dāi) are very skilful and even do 'external versions' to rotate the foetus with abnormal presentation inside the womb so that the foetus comes out easily.

The traditional healers effectively treat common ailments, set the fractured bones and even manage mental health problems.

b) Traditional Knowledge of Medicinal Plants

Soliga tribal people use more than 300 herbs for the treatment of various ailments. VGKK is doing systematic documentation of their knowledge—concepts of health, disease and healing—and manuals are being prepared in the local language to help the traditional healers. VGKK has also taken up the 'Conservation of Medicinal Plants' programme to conserve the rare and endangered species of medicinal plants in Mysore district.

An extensive field investigation into tribal medicinal practices of Bihar, West Bengal and Orissa by Sibani Mallick and Dr. K. K. Chatterjee showed that satisfactory treatment for several common ailments was being provided by the tribal doctors using local herbs. (The herbs used, methods of preparation, and routes of administration are also documented in the study report.) The ailments treated

satisfactorily were—pyrexia of unknown origin, viral fever
and malaria (76% satisfactorily treated), gastroenteric disorders (63% of cases satisfactorily treated), respiratory
diseases (63%), nonspecific arthritis (26%—and some relief
in an additional 20% of cases), dermatitis (33% satisfactory
treatment, and an additional 30% partially relieved), worm
infestation (28% cured), otitismedia (satisfactorily treated
in 48% of cases), and conjunctivitis (48%).

It was observed by the investigators as well as by
other tribal health workers that resistant dysenteries not
amenable to modern treatment were sometimes cured by
herbs provided by the Santhals of Orissa.

Tribal knowledge has been the source of many valuable medicines used today. The popularity of Reserpine
extracted from *Rauwolfia serpentina,* quinine from cinchona
bark, Ginseng and many other herbal remedies, can be
traced to chance contacts with the tribals.

In a case study which is of serious import to modern
medicine a tribal leprosy patient was instructed by the
tribal healer to live and sleep under the shade of a neem
tree and chew 21 neem leave every day for six months.
Following that, he was completely cured.

It is believed that there are many forest-based contra-
ceptives (herbal anti-fertility drugs) which tribes of certain
parts of the country may be using to prevent childbirth.
Currently studies have been undertaken to validate this
claim.

CHETNA (Centre for Health Education, Training and
Nutrition Awareness) Ahmedabad and LSPSS (Lok
Swasthya Parampara Samvardhan Samiti) Coimbatore

have done extensive studies on traditional mother-and-child healthcare practices.

Limitations of Tribal Medicine

While respecting the traditional wisdom of tribal people in healing, we should not romanticize it. There are several limitations of the system and very often tall claims are made. The tribal healer should be taught to be aware of these limitations and to know when to refer them to profes-sionals. We need to look at tribal medical care objectively and evolve a method of validating it for its efficacy. Validation has to be done based on the principles of tribal medicine and not from the framework of modern medicine.

Future Prospects of Tribal Medicine

The tribal medicine should be preserved and promoted not only to take care of the health of tribal people but also for their socio-economic development. At B. R. Hills, Mysore district, efforts are being made for 'sustainable harvesting of herbal medicines' without endangering biodiversity. The collection and processing of herbal medicine has become an important income-generating activity for the tribal people.

There is also need to protect the Intellectual Property Rights of the tribal people for their knowledge of herbal medicine, as there is a serious threat from multinational companies.

Traditional Knowledge of Nutrition

Our study of Soliga tribals in Mysore has shown the following details regarding their eating habits. They consume the following nutritious foods available in the forest:

21 species of green leaves
8 species of tubers
14 species of fruits
8 species of seeds
4 species of flowers
7 species of mushrooms
10 species of spices
4 varieties of honey

They cultivate the following food crops:

5 species of cereals
5 species of pulses
5 species of tubers
2 species of oil seeds
5 species of green leafy vegetables

1. Whole grains are powdered and consumed. The tribals also consume pulses and vegetables. The high roughage in their diet helps them in preventing colonic cancer, appendicitis and constipation.

2. The green leafy vegetables take care of their dietary needs of vitamin A and iron. Amaranthus is the most commonly used leafy vegetable—the leaves, seeds and stem are all consumed.

3. They have very little fat in their diet; hence obesity is almost unknown in the community.

4. They consume plenty of *jāmoon* (Indian black berry), which takes care of folic acid needed for the regeneration of RBCs especially in patients with sickle-cell disease, a type of anemia.

5. Even a child knows how to differentiate between edible and non-edible mushrooms. A three year child would know how to find the edible tubers in the forest.

6. They use only herbal pesticides to preserve seeds and grains. Hence their foods are totally free from chemical pesticides.

Tribal Life in Harmony with Nature

The religion and worship of the Soliga is the poetry of their life. They do not find God to be away and other-wordly but feel His presence in Nature, in the forest, in every blade of grass. Listen to this little song sung by the Soligas of Mysore:

> The Lord of Dodda Sampige*
> Do protect us!
> The creeper that hangs over the tree
> Swings gently as a cradle for Thee.

The culture of the Soliga relates to daily life. The forest is the predominant factor. No wonder those for whom the forest is life and all-in-all look upon the forest as supreme. The sky, sun, moon, and stars, air and waters, and the environment also play an important role in their life. They intuitively know that the sun is the source of all life and they worship him.

The Soligas have great reverence for trees and believe that it is a sin to cut trees. Whenever they are forced to cut a tree, they perform a small ritual; they prostrate in front of the stump and sorrowfully keep a small stone on it as testimony to the throbbing life of the tree.

In another place the description of a small bird is ecstatically sung by the tribal folk:

---

*A big Champak tree in the interior forest, worshipped by the Soligas of Mysore.

> Dear little bird, do build
> A small nest for thee!
> The Aralu* and Bende*
> Are full of thine nests.
> The Suragi* and Seege*'
> Are full of thine nests.
> Do build a small nest for three!

The tribal people are sensitive to the preservation of biodiversity. They have the knowledge of the endangered species and make efforts to protect them. The concept of sustainable harvesting of Minor Forest Produce is part of their tradition. When they harvest the root of a plant for their food or herbal medicine, they leave a part of root so that the plant can regenerate. Similarly they leave fruits and seeds in the trees so that wild animals and birds can also have their share. The tribals take only what they need for their livelihood.

Paradigm Shift in Healthcare

What India needs to day is a people-oriented, ecologically sound, sustainable, decentralized, low-cost, need-based, culturally acceptable, community-based, holistic healthcare system through an empowering process.

The Medical Care System of tribals in India has several of the above characteristics inherent in it. It could be integrated into the primary healthcare in tribal areas. This would, however, necessitate a paradigm shift in healthcare in India.

---

*Names of trees; incidentally, songs like this help tribal children learn the names of birds and trees.

BIBLIOGRAPHY

1. *Soliga Tribe & Its Stride* (B. R. Hills, Mysore: Vivekananda Girijana Kalyana Kendra).
2. Dr. Ashok Sahani & Dr. Sudha Kshirasagar, *Health and Development of the Tribal People in India* (Bangalore: ISHA).
3. *Tribal Health in India.* Edited by Dr. Bhupinder Singh and Neeti Mahanti.
4. *Her Healing Heritage* (Ahmedabad: CHETNA).

15

Holistic Health in Home Care Nursing

NANCY BROOKS

Home health nurses have learned that to help means to listen and to take the time to allow trust to be established. A nurse may be asked (by a physician, a family member or concerned neighbour or friend) to evaluate a patient in the home. However, the patient is 'in charge' at home and is under no obligation to be evaluated or examined. They may refuse the service. It's a choice. Many feel that to be in one's own home means to be independent. Even if we are not able to live alone without assistance from others, we have rights and can make choices. Sometimes refusing to accept a service or to comply with 'doctor's orders' seems like one of the few choices we have left. In the hospital or clinic setting, the patient is not 'in charge,' the staff is. The doctor makes the decisions and the patient then decides, consciously or unconsciously, to follow the instructions or to forget them. Everyone's goal is the same. Getting better, feeling better, finding out what's wrong.

Today not everyone agrees on what's best in health-care. Patients often complain that 'no one has time to listen' or 'they don't really care.' Unfortunately in today's hurried healthcare world, even the most compassionate person may not have the luxury of listening to the patient's complete story. The system has not taken into consideration the spiritual, emotional and mental needs of the patient. Time, money and the scientific method seem to be more impor-tant.

Attitude Adjustment

Our bodies have an innate wisdom, an ability to heal when we provide the proper atmosphere, physically, emo-tionally and mentally. An illness may not be a choice, but how we respond to it, is. Our response is often the key to healing. A change of attitude is possibly more important for some of us than a change in diet or life-style. The potential for healing is vastly improved when our thoughts are 'I can' rather than 'I can't' or 'it won't work anyway' or 'it's too much trouble.' When we allow for the possibility of improve-ment or new learning, it can change our life as well as our health. Seeing options in our everyday life is critical to our health and well-being. When we see our options as being limited we feel trapped, but allowing ourselves a wide range of choices helps us feel free. 'Choice also strengthens our immune system,' according to Carl Hammerschlag, a physician in Arizona who works with Native Americans.

Our Bodies and Our Minds

Sometimes our gastrointestinal (GI) tract is a window on our emotions. We're not always aware of feeling trapped or depressed or stressed, but we are aware if our stomach sends a message or distress signal. For those of us who experience emotions in a visceral way, it can lead to physical problems if the signals are not respected and if we fail to make changes. When strong emotions are felt, our GI tract is often a barometer, it gives us advance warning that we need to pay attention and make adjustments in our attitude or in our behaviour. If we repeatedly ignore these signals, we take the chance of missing important information our body is trying to transmit.

We can prevent more critical physical problems if we heed the warning signs and change our behaviour and/or our thinking. Carl Hammerschlag says, 'Our bodies and our minds see things in different ways. When we ignore our bodies' messages and think we know what is wrong, our bodies are forced to send stronger messages to us to feel.' Feeling our feelings gives us the information we need to stay healthy. If my stomach is my barometer and I'm avoiding 'taking action' on an issue that is important in my life, my stomach may remind me. It's sensible to ask myself, 'What am I avoiding?' Sometimes it may be that I'm avoiding looking at a problem that I have relegated to the 'it's not *that* important' file. A part of us is aware even when we've rationalized an issue. Our feeling body knows more than our thinking mind and is able to access the information for us. Listening to this information by quieting the mind is a learned skill and, when practised, serves us well.

Insight into Action

Of all the actions we can take to improve or maintain our health, 'right thinking' is the most valuable. How we respond to others and how we feel is something we can control. Being obsessed with or holding on to fear or doubt weakens our minds and our bodies. What we think about affects how we feel physically, mentally and emotionally.

Taking care of ourselves is our job in life. Dealing with uncomfortable issues that make a difference to the quality of our life is our responsibility. Issues such as control, anger and fear are real and our bodies respond in ways to notify us that we need to take some kind of action. Sometimes this means rephrasing our thoughts in positive ways that allows us the possibility of growth and enlightenment.

Two of my patients (96 years of age), that I think of as role models, tell me that their 'secret of longevity' is 'because I live without extremes, I try to do everything in moderation' and 'I have a very strong spiritual orientation and lot of support from my church.' Many of the patients that have been the most contented with their lives talk about looking on the bright side and keeping interested in the world around them. These are the patients who don't seem to suffer from depression and loneliness and isolation.

Changes in Healthcare

Why did holistic health come into prominence and why is home healthcare ever more popular? Both appeal to us because they seem to put us 'in charge' of our own healthcare decisions. The days of the old country doctor who had time to listen and discuss our concerns are over. Few healthcare practitioners have the luxury of time. For the elderly or seriously ill patients, listening to what they have to say is often critical to the outcome of their treatment. Being rushed doesn't encourage confidences or a relaxed atmosphere where trust can be established and where learning can occur. The relaxation response is an integral part of healing, which usually begins with the initial interview between a patient and the healthcare practitioner. The time spent together can be a part of the healing process when compassion, support and listening attentively are part of the patient/practitioner interaction.

Most of us know when someone cares and when they're listening to us. They make eye contact and they don't interrupt or put words in our mouth. They don't deny our feelings or our complaints by trying to minimize them or explain them away. They don't tell us we shouldn't be feeling the way we're feeling. Albert Schweitzer said, 'It is more important for the doctor to know the patient who has the disease than to know the disease that has the patient.'

Responsibility and Patient's Role

Patients who ask questions about medications, tests, treatments, and symptoms seem to do better than patients who accept whatever is offered without question. They're part of the solution rather than asking to be 'taken care of' or 'cured' by the physician or healthcare practitioner. A patient with positive expectations who is a partner in his or her own care usually has an easier time with all phases of medical care. When we 'turn ourselves over to the doctor' we are not part of the solution, we become part of the problem.

Some physicians, such as Dr. Christiane Northrup, an obstetrician and gynecologist in Maine, are holistically oriented. They are comfortable with supporting patients who want to play an active part in their care. They are open, honest and nonthreatened by things they weren't taught in medical school.

The patient's role has been changing radically. As a home health nurse I have seen some of these changes that have occurred. Patients and their families or caregivers have been forced to take more responsibility due to the changes in the healthcare delivery system. They can no longer rely on their physician for medical management. Unlike the old country doctor, today's busy physician isn't able to see the whole picture. A patient may see more than one doctor and take several different medications. For safety and good management, one doctor must be in charge if medications are prescribed by several different doctors.

If elderly people have been hospitalized, they may have been discharged home too soon. Often before they are able to return to their previous activities without some outside help. They may have new medications or changes in old medications or a new diagnosis such as adult-onset diabetes (common in the elderly). They are often unaware that drugs are processed differently in the aging body and probably won't report symptoms unless they are obvious. Most patients I have evaluated at home are eager for information and frequently unaware of the details of their diagnosis, medications and diet restrictions. If they do have adult-onset diabetes, they may not realize how it can affect them and simply feel their 'sugar is a little high.' They may not have received proper information and therefore don't take diabetes as seriously as they should. Diabetes mellitus can cause permanent damage to the blood vessels and nerves without any obvious symptoms. It is the patients' responsibility, when given a new prescription or diagnosis, to ask some basic questions and get answers. This isn't easy, but they cannot expect their doctor to be responsible for all aspects of their health.

Changes in Expectations

The holistic and the traditional medical models are almost exact opposites. Some of us believe they are compatible and can complement one another and become integrated to form a third healthcare system that honours the full spectrum of the human being. This change would encourage the shift in the balance of power that seems to be growing. The strongest message of the holistic health movement is that physicians are not responsible for the quality of a patient's health.

Not everyone is ready or willing to accept changes that are occurring in healthcare. Accepting the responsibility for oneself and the power that comes with that responsibility may be difficult for some. The patient knows best what he or she can have faith in and accept. Whatever the choice, it is of the utmost importance that family and friends support the choice, regardless of their own personal preferences. Ultimately, we are the ones that live with our choices and the results of those choices.

Allowing a patient to continue a lifestyle that may be self-destructive is difficult but sometimes the only choice left to the care provider and the patient's family. One can offer options, but the final decision is always with the patient. To be supported in whatever decision is made is the patient's right also. This is not easy for the care provider who sees the detrimental results of that choice. Ultimately we all need to be supported in our choices. To be trusted to make the right decision for ourselves, even when it may not look right to others, is empowering. Peter and Elizabeth Albright in *Body, Mind, & Spirit* state that 'responsibility for healthcare rests in the patient's hands because that is where the knowledge and control of the variables lie (diet, stress, exercise, genetics, emotion, medication).'

Changes in Needs

Holistic healthcare is sometimes referred to as 'alternative care.' A more descriptive term might be 'complementary healthcare.' Much of what is available holistically isn't an alternative to traditional medicine but an addition to it.

Traditional medicine works well in certain areas such as emergency situations (trauma, cardiac arrest, fractures and infectious diseases). Complementary therapies such as acupuncture, acupressure, imagery, massage, relaxation and meditation work well with stress, skin problems, gastrointestinal disorders, and heart disease. The family doctor of a century ago was really a holistic physician. He knew the family and was often able to understand the *whole* person, not just the original complaint. This is something conventional medicine has lost.

The rapid growth of the holistic health field indicates that our needs have changed in fundamental ways. Traditional medicine and the current healthcare system cannot adequately meet these needs. Changes are also occurring in how people define responsibility. Patients who feel empowered view the medical community in a different way. They question, which means that the strongly held position of authority by traditional medicine no longer exists. More people are recognizing that their own life stresses have contributed to the creation of their illness. Pythagoras said that the most divine art was that of healing. And if the healing art is most divine, it must occupy itself with the soul as well as with the body. As Apollonius of Tyana said, 'No creature can be sound so long as the higher part in it is sickly.'

Elderhood

Healthy, elderly people have less need for medical investigation and treatment than they do for reassurance, information and advice that will help them maintain and improve their health. It's even more important, when giving information, to listen to the elderly. Their beliefs and attitudes are more influential than medical evidence. It's also helpful to be as brief as possible, keep it simple, be clear, be specific, keep it relevant, and reinforce by summarizing and writing down important points of information.

A vision test is recommended every two years, unless problems arise sooner. Screening for hypertension (high blood pressure), osteoporosis and cancer is good preventive medicine. Early identification of alcohol use, depression, dementia, dental problems, hearing or vision deficits can often save needless worry and grief. Fear of being 'put in a nursing home' prevents many elderly people from dealing with such concerns. In order to stay independent and experience quality of life we need to share our fears and concerns with someone we can trust. Sharing a worrisome burden can often help reduce anxiety and put things in perspective. Complex medical problems can often be avoided if diagnosed and treated early.

Normal Aging

Normal aging does not have to involve dizziness, confusion, memory loss or incontinence. Cataracts on the eyes, skin diseases, and depression should not be expected as a part of growing older either. Illness or disease is not a fundamental part of aging. Body systems do slow down. Old age does involve a dimming of vision, hearing, taste, and smell, but these are gradual changes and can be dealt with as they occur. Older people who are forgetful have *not* lost their memory. It is important to distinguish clearly between forgetfulness and memory loss. Losing a purse or car keys all the time is forgetfulness, not knowing that they are lost or shy you need them is memory loss. Forgetfulness also involves remembering an occasion but not all the details.

An older person who has physical problems (possibly undiagnosed) and some sensory losses will have a much more difficult time coping with memory problems. Unless a sudden onset of memory loss occurs, the memory losses of dementia are barely distinguishable from the forgetfulness and absentmindedness that everyone experiences.

The following questions from Carboline Rob's *The Caregiver's Guide* can help assess whether or not a professional evaluation is needed: (1) Does the older person forget well-known information? (2) Does the older person repeatedly totally lose recall of recent events, such as your visit the day before, or the food just served at lunch? (3) Are there signs of difficulty in doing tasks that have always been done well, such as reading a book, knitting a sweater, or balancing the cheque-book? (4) Has forgetfulness begun to cause significant troubles with safety, such as driving on the wrong side of the road, or leaving the cooking gas on repeatedly?

The Bottom Line

When we, as patients, take responsibility for our experiences and decisions in healthcare, we will feel empowered and 'in charge' of our lives. Choosing to become a partner in our healing means listening to our inner guidance. To quote Albert Schweitzer, 'It's a trade secret, but I'll tell you anyway. All healing is self-healing.'

Taking responsibility for one's own health and wellbeing is a big step. Some of us never make the transition. Until we take the most important step of all, a change in attitude, we won't be fully in charge of our own lives.

16
Kai-igaku: The Way of Universal Medicine

RYOSUKE URYU

I offer my warmest greetings, in friendship and solidarity, to all who are working so hard for the sake of life on Earth. The following is a basic introduction to *kai-igaku* ('Comfortable Medicine') and a message from the World Kai-Igaku Network, set up on the basis of free and equal exchange of experience and mutual aid between people who wish to make radical changes in conventional medicine, so that the vital power and ability for self-healing of individuals and the planet can manifest themselves in freedom.

We seek to change orthodox medicine in the following ways:

(1) By rescuing our one-sided medical service, which believes science and technology have all the answers, and neglects what science' cannot prove, and transforming it into one that is more aware of the natural laws of universal life and capable of making correct use of the phenomena of life: life energy, 'ki', and the body's natural powers of recovery.

(2) By abolishing animal vivisection, which is an extreme expression of human conceit that we have the right to use all the life forms and resources of the earth entirely for ourselves. Medicine must be a pillar of the new ecology, where all beings live together in mutual respect and enjoyment.

(3) By forming a network of people who are aware of the roots of medicine (healing) and regaining control of our medical service which, protected by the Medical Act, dominates people and operates in secret behind closed doors.

The word *kai-igaku* means 'comfortable medicine.' The universe, nature, or God accords to us and every living being a natural term of life wherein we can live and die comfortably. Every living being is created to live in paradise, with the sole purpose of living happily in paradise together. The phenomena of life can be defined as a constant forward movement, always striving for comfort and avoiding discomfort.

The source of the universal law of comfort is not accessible to the present knowledge of humanity, and all we can do is to express our gratitude. The roots of all disease lie in breaking the universal law of comfort and living 'uncomfortably' or in an uncomfortable environment. Recovery from disease only means starting to move in the direction of comfort, which is what the body and mind really desire, and adapting ourselves to the simple but inescapable laws of comfort laid down over billions of years of evolution.

The profoundest strength of medicine (healing) is the patient's own vital power. All forms of medicine, including modern Western medicine and oriental medicine, must ultimately depend on this universal life power which is really nothing other than nature's power of healing. The role of the doctor or therapist is to tell the patient the origin of his or her illness, to stimulate the patient to turn towards comfort, and to aid very slightly in the natural process of recovery from disease.

We have helped in the recovery of people with all kinds of chronic and so-called incurable illnesses, including cancer, and found it is not difficult work, or the specialized province of medicine: on the contrary, the marvellous healing power of nature manifests itself in the home, at the office, in school, wherever people are free and equal in the 'magnetic field' of a community, and exchange kind looks with each other. Medicine is by the people, for the people, and of the people.

There is nothing difficult about it. All we have to do is turn away from the false comforts of modern civilization in which the cerebral cortex is immersed, and think of what each and every one of our cells most wants for its comfort, and what food and drink would make us feel best. Then, listening to the body, we should act on it. (It is easy to read the body by using the 'life energy test' described below.)

There are certain essential activities that human beings have to engage in to stay alive: breathing, eating and drinking, physical activity and mental activity. A comfortable balance between these four activities and the environment is the basic principle for recovery from disease. The environment itself poses a serious problem which we will have to solve over the next several hundred years, but we can start practising the above four activities at once. And in all of them we find the simple but inescapable universal law of comfort at work.

Two methods are used in the practice of *kai-igaku*. *Sotai-Ho* (Sotai Method), based on the universal law of comfort, involves moving the body slowly in a comfortable direction and removing any physical distortions in the motor system. *Soto Medicine* (Synthetic Medicine) is concerned with adjusting the temperature of the liver, kidney, spleen and thymus to a comfortable level.

To identify illnesses I use the 'life energy test.' When a few grams of pressure is applied to the surface of the skin and a variety of samples placed in contact with the body, certain changes are seen in the tension held between the fingers. It is a simple, non-intrusive technique which enables us to identify abnormalities in the internal organs, to detect bacterial infections and the presence of cancer, and to determine the appropriateness of drugs and diet.

Made up of these three systems, *kai-igaku* is in fact very easy and 'comfortable,' and the basics can be learned in 30 to 50 hours by people with no conventional medical background.

Kai-igaku is a system that rationally integrates with oriental medicine, psychology, the brain sciences and immunology.

What Are the Fundamental Laws?

There are many possibilities available to us in life, but for a minimal level of existence, there are a few absolute essentials: breathing, eating, (physical) movement and (mental/spiritual) thought.

ABSOLUTE REQUIREMENTS
& THEIR BALANCE WITH THE ENVIRONMENT

(Input)   (Output)
Breathing   Movement
Eating   Thought
Environment

Breathing and eating are the means by which we absorb energy from the universe: input. Movement and thought are the means by which we burn the energy we absorb from the universe: output. You cannot ask others to do these things for you. You have to take responsibility for them yourself. There are many ways of acting but the choice is yours. And a comfortable balance between the above four activities and the environment is the key to recovery from malignant disease. The more serious the disease, the more you must reflect on and consider this fundamental principle. So long as you resist this principle of balance and continue to live an uncomfortable life, there will be an inclination to disease.

The environment surrounding the four activities includes not only the physical environment but human relations at home, school or workplace. It also includes the relations between human beings and other creatures, and

ultimately our relationship with the whole universe. All
these elements interact and support one another, and all of
them are equally important. Some people select only one of
the four activities and concentrate only on breathing, for
example. They emphasize breathing exercises but don't devote much attention to proper food or proper movement. It
is possible to make up for deficiencies in other areas by
concentrating on only one, but this requires a lot of effort.
People with special ability can do this, but most ordinary
people cannot. Instead, I suggest you aim for a 60% score in
each of the four areas, and adapt yourself to the law in a
calm and joyful way, without going overboard in any one
area. This is more in keeping with the principles of life.

The five elements—breathing, eating, movement,
thought, and environment—interlock with each other
synergistically. Energy taken in is balanced with energy
expended. 'The phenomenon of life is a phenomenon of balance' (Hashimoto Keizo). There is a dynamic equilibrium
between the attainment of comfort in each of the five elements. Life functions by always moving in the direction of
comfort so as to maintain a comfortable balance between
one's own territory and that of others (homeostasis).

True health is to be able to live and die freely and
joyfully amid absolute otherness. We can only live freely
and playfully with a sense of inexpressible gratitude for the
chance gift of life. To live in accord with the basic will of the
universe we must let others (all living beings) do as they
will. The pursuit of comfort is an absolute. And comfort is
synergistic. We must build a system where all beings joyfully coexist in 'comfort' in both senses.

Living creatures can only live by taking life. All living creatures give themselves to sustain others' spheres of comfort. But what are we to make of human beings who only take and give nothing in return? What are our lives if we can only live by killing other creatures? The idea of coexisting with all living beings is just a conceit unless we make full use of the life that we do take, leaving nothing to waste. In this sense cooking is a deep philosophy.

We must train ourselves to see through the superficial 'comforts' of modern civilization. We must create a mutually supportive space where we can learn the real comfort that every cell in our bodies cries out for, rather than the shallow comfort imagined by the cerebral cortex.

The Law of Comfortable Breathing

The basic idea is to exhale more and more. Try to breathe out completely, any time during the day. As you exhale, inhalation will occur naturally. Whenever we make a sudden physical movement we either exhale or hold our breath. Try to exhale symbols of evil such as prestige, money and power.

The Law of Comfortable Eating

Our staple food should be unpolished cereals (brown rice, wheat, millet, farmyard millet) and a large variety and quantity of vegetables (500 grams per day), always including carrots and pumpkins. We also need a well-balanced intake of seaweed, small fish, eggs and milk with up to two meals a day. We should try to live in harmony with the micro-organisms of our intestines. Fermented foods such as miso (soybean paste), soy sauce and fermented soybeans are important foods. Eat happily, together with other people, and chew each mouthful 50 times, even when you are busy.

The Law of Comfortable Physical Movement

Human joints move in eight directions. Try each of the eight directions, then move slowly in the most comfortable direction while exhaling. When you reach the limits of the comfortable position, inhale. Then release all the tension in your body with a single exhalation. This will remove the distortion in your body. The technique is known as *sotai*.

Another law to be applied in everyday life is that of maintaining stability in the body by properly adjusting the centre of gravity. When bending, the body weight should be shifted to the opposite side from that on which you are bending. When twisting, the body weight should lean in the same direction as the twist. When extending, the body weight should remain on the side that is being extended.

The Law of Comfortable Mental Activity

Do what you want to do, comfortably. But while doing so, you should also give others the freedom to do what they want, otherwise your actions will be irrational and unethical. 'Others' means all other creatures. When you need to escape, escape in the most comfortable direction. Sometimes you have to run away fast, or your mind and body will be destroyed.

Thus we have to adapt ourselves to life's laws of comfort and keep our minds and bodies in their best condition. Then we can confront the most difficult of challenges like healing the environment and creating a heaven on earth, where all beings can enjoy life together in mutual respect.

The Law of Comfortable Environment

We should escape from any environment that is uncomfortable. This could mean taking time off work, changing jobs or moving house, leaving home, living apart, getting married or divorced. It could mean travelling or recuperating elsewhere. Of course, the greatest problem we are faced with is the ailing global environment—which we cannot run away from.

Human beings have exhausted the earth and virtually destroyed it. What people can immediately do is reinvigorate themselves by following the five principles of comfort. This will give them a base from which to find a way out of the crisis. We have to set a limit on the amount of resources that each individual can consume. We have to rethink what is meant by quality of life and quality of comfort. The time has come for us to ask what is the 'comfort' all of our cells are crying out for, and to set the whole world—people's environment as well as the way they breathe, eat, think, and move—on a path towards comfort.

For the lazy, there are five quick and easy ways to put the principles of comfort into practice: (1) Massage of the thymus, (2) 'Goldfish' exercise, (3) Sotai exercises: heel stretches, body twist with knees bent, neck stretches, (4) drink a glass of your own urine first thing each morning, and (5) immerse only the lower half of the body when taking a bath.

Inclination to Disease

When the Laws of Comfort are violated, the body becomes fragile. Stress from outside, in the form of injury, germs and viruses, fatigue or mental pressure, then results in an inclination towards disease. If the five elements of life, the four activities and the environment, are out of balance, illness will arise.

The first symptoms of disease manifest as sensory abnormalities such as numbness and pain. If you work immediately to correct that imbalance, you can prevent deterioration and get back on the road to health. In many cases we find illness is accompanied by physical distortion of the body, and here *sotai* is very effective.

Many people, when they are ill, continue to claim they are healthy, and persevere through sensations of numbness and pain. People who do not recognize these danger signals in their bodies advance from the sensory stage of pain and numbness to the stage of functional disorder and abnormalities such as, for example, chronic constipation or diarrhoea, frozen shoulder, poor eyesight, and skin complaints. Even at this stage, however, some people insist they are still healthy. And unfortunately, conventional medical diagnostic tests cannot detect these sensory or functional abnormalities.

The next stage of disease is structural abnormality such as, for example, stomach ulcers, cancer and hepatitis. By the time liver disease reaches the third stage, two thirds of the liver has already been damaged. The liver is a fantastic organ that can operate even when 70–80% of it has been destroyed. Some people still fail to recognize the danger signals in the third stage of disease, continuing to insist they are healthy while heading towards death.

We must control ourselves in such a way that sensory disorders do not arise and our body and mind function pleasantly and comfortably. At the least, we should notice any inclination to disease while it is still at the first stage of sensory abnormality, and make an effort to get back to normal by reorganizing our lives. 'Effort' and 'reorganizing' sound negative, seeming to involve coercion, but how fortunate we are because, here too, all we have to do is seek out the most comfortable direction and keep going only in that direction!

The body has amazing powers of recuperation. There are cases of cancer patients whose tumors were discovered during surgery to have metastasized all over their bodies, but went on to make 'miraculous' recoveries. As long as there is a breath of life in a patient, there is a possibility of reversing the process of disease. This must always be kept in mind.

17
Self-Healing

NARAS BHAT

Self-healing refers to the process of repairing, rebuilding, and balancing our mind-body. When we are wounded by an injury, infection, or degeneration, the wound is deeper than our afflicted body part. The wound affects our body, mind, and soul. Our mind and body meet at the level of messenger molecules between two cells. There is a continuous exchange of information between our cells to heal or remain wounded. The doctor may give antibiotics or do surgery, but our tissue has to heal by itself. In fact, the antibiotic proven to be the strongest does not work at times because the mind-body has lost the power to heal.

All healing has the final pathway of self-healing or self-regulation. In any system of self-regulation we have to have the feedback and feed-forward of information. The science of regulation by feedback and feed-forward is called cybernetics. This is like our home heating system, the heat from the furnace is fed-forward to the temperature gauge and the on-off switch which give the feedback to the furnace. Self-healing requires similar measurements, monitoring, and modifying of the healing forces. In summary, healing by self-regulation has two parts: mindfulness to measure and monitor the processes of our mind-body, and action plan to modify.

What Is Heart-Centred Living?

The centre of our action is our heart, both metaphorically and anatomically. Our heart is 60 times stronger as an electrical generator compared to the brain. The heart is the big brother and the brain is the little brother. All activities of the mind-body pivot around the central powerhouse —our heart. We have two different existences, head-centred and heart-centred. The new science of cardio-neuro-immunology has clarified that self-healing requires a cardiocentric attention. If we live with our head-centred script, we are judgmental. If we live with heart-centred caring love, we are incapable of developing any enemy. But in modern life, we have flip-flopped both the scripts. We spend most of our waking hours in judging others with the hidden question of 'what is in it for me.'

Why Learn About Self-Healing?

The skill of self-healing gives us three distinct benefits: stress control, shifting the momentum from degenerative afflictions and aging to regeneration, and achieving our maximal self with creativity. We can go to the best doctor in town and get the best pills, but the final healing has to happen by the forces of nature acting on our mind-body.

What Are Our Choices in Healing?

If we have a serious degenerative disorder such as heart disease or cancer, we have two choices to heal ourselves:

1. Conventional Medicine (*external pharmacy of 'pill power,'* surgery, radiation, etc)
2. Alternative Healing (*internal pharmacy of 'skill power,'* mind-body healing, transpersonal healing, etc)

All healing has the final pathway of self-healing.

If we have chosen the best doctor and best hospital in town, are we assured of the maximal healing power? The answer is a clear no, because a breakthrough scientific research has now shown that all external drugs and procedures have to work through the 'internal pharmacy' of healing chemicals produced inside our body. Invoking this internal healing power is called life-style modification. It is a skill. Skill by definition is the ability to do something well. If we are skilful in invigorating the internal healing chemicals, our need for external drug is minimized.

Why Focus on Internal Healing Power?

The human body has its own resilience or healing power just like the lower animals. But the excessive focus on external events of daily activities and an achievement-oriented culture keep our stress arousal level unnaturally high. This releases chemicals such as cortisol, adrenalin, and noradrenaline leading to suppression of the immune system and weakening of our healing power. Optimal healing requires us to get away from this frenzy and vigilance. This diversion from a stress-aroused state is called altered state. In order to heal better, we should be able to enter into the altered state.

What Is an Altered State?

An altered state is a state different from the normal awakened state. We have three states of consciousness: normal awakened state (*jāgrata*), sleep with dream (*svapna*), sleep without dream (*suṣupti*). There is a higher 'state' also, which we might call the meditative state. It is common sense that restful sleep is conducive to healing. Can we recall the twilight zone of just falling asleep and just waking up? This interface of entering into sleep is called hypnagoic state, and exiting from sleep is called hypnapompic state. The twilight state has alpha theta brain waves compared to beta waves during awakened state. The meditative state is the same as the twilight state, except that we enter it and exit from it by choice. The meditative state allows our mind and body to talk to each other.

In summary, our stressful life-style does not allow us to enter the altered state of sleep, daydream, and meditation, to heal by proper mind-body communication.

What Is Systems Concept of Healing?

Medical science divides the body into systems, such as the cardiovascular system, digestive system, nervous system, etc. There are qualified specialists in each system to diagnose and treat us with allopathic drugs. But when it comes to healing, we need two additional systems: our belief system in the type of medicine, and our self-regulation of internal healing system.

What Are the Three Eras of Medicine?

Modern allopathic medicine, or 'physical medicine,' belongs to the first era. It is based on the 17th century logic given by René Descartes. It creates dichotomy between mind and body. Mind is 'disembodied thought' and body is 'mindless machine.' Treating a disease is like fixing a part of a machine. Either we repair the broken part or replace it. Each part or organ is treated as an independent piece. Unfortunately, human body parts are interdependent, not independent. The organ specialists, high-tech diagnostic equipment, and 'magic bullet' drugs are the markers of this era of medicine.

The second era of medicine refers to 'mind-body medicine.' It became popular in the 1960s with the advent of meditation, imagery, hypnosis, and biofeedback. Here the goal is to invoke the messenger molecules to accomplish the healing process. Mind and body connect to each other by these messenger molecules. Examples of mind-body healing models are: Dean Ornish's reversing heart disease, Simonton and Siegel's cancer healing by diet, meditation and imagery, and Eugene Peniston's addiction healing by electronic meditation of brain wave feedback.

The third era of medicine refers to 'transpersonal medicine.' It became popular in 1990s with the advent of group support and spirituality to heal. Examples of transpersonal healing models are: The Spiegel study of breast cancer patients at Stanford, doubling their longevity by group support, and Randolph Byrd study at San Francisco, proving the power of prayer to heal heart patients.

Why Should We Take Advantage of All the Three Eras?

Using only the 'pill-power' of allopathic medicine is being like a carpenter who uses only a hammer and nail compared to another carpenter who uses the hammer, nail, chisel, saw, and a measuring tape. There is a saying: if you have a hammer in hand, everything looks like a nail. A narrow-focused allopathic approach tries to fix the chemistry of the body with external drugs. If there are side effects from one drug, a second drug is given to counteract it.

How Can We Get Motivated to Use the Three Eras?

Our motivation is based on our belief system and expectancy. In modern times, the most powerful way to change the belief system is by scientific evidence verified by our own personal experience. Breakthrough medical research has shown that mind-body healing and the transpersonal process of healing are scientifically validated by proven models. In my heart disease reversal clinic, we measure the blood cholesterol, blood pressure, and heart rate before and after using our mind-body healing tools, and we have documented dramatic improvement in hundreds of our patients.

Why the Conventional Allopathic Doctor and Hospitals Ignore Mind-body Medicine?

The conventional practitioners of medicine have three reasons to ignore the mind-body healing methods: (1) pharmaceutical and insurance industry controls the 'healing business,' (2) high-tech gadgets and computers focus on organ systems of body, like parts of a machine, and (3) the standards of law, science, and business ethics require the medical practitioners to conform to the prevailing system. The laws of the land and the laws of Nature are two different domains. Let us now focus on the laws of Nature, regardless of which land we live in.

Natural Healing: Tonic vs Toxic Factors

The word 'healing' means to make whole. Healing is the use of inner power or resources to balance and harmonize the mind-body by restoring its self-regulation and wholeness. The essence of self-regulation is mindful monitoring and self-directed modification in behaviour. The outside drugs and food have to work through our 'internal pharmacy' to heal us. We can also modify our 'internal pharmacy' by knowing our mind-body connections. Healing can be natural and spontaneous if we allow it to happen without disturbing the laws of Nature.

Our body has the power to heal and regenerate right from the level of DNA, the genetic master code. If one strand of DNA is broken, it replicates the original form. Compare a piece of ivy vine: if we cut it and plant it, it grows back. But if we keep cutting the ivy plant to smaller and smaller pieces, a point comes when it stops replicating. Similarly, a denatured DNA stops replicating. Besides replicating, the DNA transcribes and translates vital messages to other tissues through messenger molecules. Mind and body meet at the level of these messenger molecules. New research has shown that our genes in the DNA are not entirely inherited destiny. One third of our over 100,000 genes are housekeeping genes, their behaviour is a miniature reflection of our behaviour in general.

The factors that promote healing are called tonics, as contrasted with toxins that slow down healing. The external tonics include drugs, low-fat, plant-based foods, vitamins, minerals, and herbs. The external toxins include pollutants, fatty animal foods, pesticides, and herbicides. At

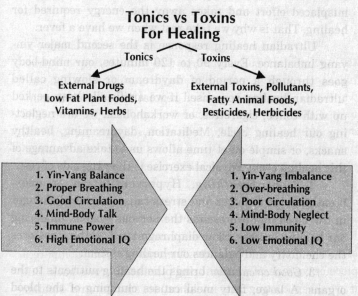

Tonics vs Toxins For Healing

Tonics

Toxins

External Drugs
Low Fat Plant Foods,
Vitamins, Herbs

External Toxins, Pollutants,
Fatty Animal Foods,
Pesticides, Herbicides

1. Yin-Yang Balance
2. Proper Breathing
3. Good Circulation
4. Mind-Body Talk
5. Immune Power
6. High Emotional IQ

1. Yin-Yang Imbalance
2. Over-breathing
3. Poor Circulation
4. Mind-Body Neglect
5. Low Immunity
6. Low Emotional IQ

the atomic level, the tonic factors produce antioxidants that counteract the harmful free radicals. The free radicals either go on a nuclear war with the cell nucleus, denaturing DNA and altering the immune system which can cause infections or cancer. The second kind of free-radical war is the membrane war which denatures the connective tissue membranes and causes degenerative aging, including wrinkling of skin, hardening of arteries, and heart disease.

The specific laws of nature for healing are summarized in six points below:

1. *Yin-Yang balance.* Everything in life has opposites: yin-yang. The most common yin-yang imbalance is stress arousal. Stress arousal increases the adrenaline and cortisol levels which suppress the immune system. Stress is misplaced effort and takes away the energy required for healing. That is why we take rest when we have a fever.

Ultradian healing response is the second major yin-yang imbalance. Every 90 to 120 minutes, our mind-body goes through a period of daydream or slowing called 'ultradian healing response.' If we artificially keep perked up with coffee, cigarettes, or workaholism, we are neglecting our healing cycle. Meditation, daydreaming, healthy snacks, or simple quiet time allows us to take advantage of this healing cycle. Physical exercise is the yang side of rest.

2. *Proper breathing.* Hyperventilation or over-breathing due to anger and stress causes chemical changes in the blood and overexcites the nervous system, hindering our healing process. Slow diaphragmatic breathing restores the chemistry and balances our healing system.

3. *Good circulation* brings the healing nutrients to the organs. A large, fatty meal causes clumping of the blood

cells and blocks off several small arteries, thereby damaging the tissues. In fact, one to ten hours after a large fatty meal, anginal chest pain or heart attack incidence is increased. Another major factor in constricting our blood vessels is stress arousal with the release of toxic levels of adrenaline compounds.

4. *Mind-body dialogue.* Our mind and body are connected by the hard wire of the nervous system, liquid media of neuro-transmitters, immune transmitters and hormones, and the vibrational whisper of brain waves and heart waves. We have a continuous dialogue with our body by our self-talk, or symbols such as imagery, dreams, daydreams and metaphors. We can enhance our mind-body communication in altered states of consciousness such as meditation, sleep, biofeedback, and hypnosis.

5. *Our immune power* is increased by enhancing our vertical intimacy with ourselves and horizontal intimacy with others. Vertically, we learn our own mind-body dynamics, and connect to our higher self with hope and spirituality. Food affects our immune system. Psycho-neuro-immunology is the new science of mind-body connection. Recently, cardio-neuro-immunology has shown that our heart is the control centre of our body and emotions have a pivotal role in our immune power.

Helplessness is a state of immune suppression that occurs after a major setback such as failing a test, having an accident, or facing the diagnosis of a catastrophic illness such as heart disease or cancer. It is like a rapid that puts us in a whirlpool and we cannot get out with our usual swimming skills. We learn to believe that our failure is permanent and pervasive in all fields of life. The antidote to helplessness is optimism. We can learn to be optimistic by engaging in any activity with a state of flow. Flow means we do some activity in which we have challenge, control, and commitment to engross with pleasure. For example, if we have failed in a geography test, we can go and boost our immune system by a flow activity in tennis on a regular basis. If we are depressed after a heart attack, we can take up a new challenging hobby. In my heart clinic, biofeedback to manage our own mind-body self-regulation, and learning the art of caring love by heart-centred living are two power-tools we use to get a person out of the state of helplessness.

Horizontally, we can learn empathy and caring love. This requires a heart-centred, non-judgmental way of life. We improve our horizontal intimacy by caring love and sharing our emotions. First we understand our own emotions and disclose it to our partner. With horizontal intimacy, we learn that people are not difficult but different.

6. *Emotional IQ.* Just like our intelligence quotient (IQ) that measures our scholastic excellence, our ability to measure, monitor, and modify our emotions has direct bearing on our healing process. Our emotional intelligence is based on two factors: vertical intimacy of understanding and modifying our body reactions to different emotions, and horizontal intimacy of caring for others and sharing our feelings with them.

What makes us thrive—our scholastic excellence or emotional intelligence? A recent Harvard research looked at ninety-five people who graduated in the 1940s and found that their academic excellence and SAT score had no relationship to their success, health, happiness, or a balanced relationship in life. Another study at Massachusetts looked at 450 sons of immigrants with low academic excellence in school, but with more fulfilment and balance in life.

IQ or intelligence quotient refers to our ability to process information and problem solving. IQ is a left-brained, linear-thinking with linguistic, mathematical power. It is measured by SAT or IQ tests.

Emotional IQ is right-brained, nonlinear-thinking with artistic, intuitive power. It is measured with emotional IQ factors. Recently Peter Salovy from Yale University, and the *New York Times* columnist Daniel Goleman have shed fresh light on the area of emotional intelligence. The five components of emotional IQ are:

a) *Measuring and monitoring our mind-body dialogue.* Becoming familiar with the feeling as it develops and with how our own body responds to each feeling; how a particular emotion affects our muscle tension, emotional sweating, heart rate, breathing, digestive system, sleep pattern, restless mind, and so on; which part of our physiology responds to which emotion first—all this is called our own physiological signature or physiological fingerprints unique to us. We have two basic emotions, viz. love and fear. Out of fear, we develop anger, guilt, and sadness.

b) *Modifying our feelings.* Karl Marx once said, 'If you want to learn how the government works, try to change it.' If we want to learn about our emotions, we must try changing them. We cannot change a feeling by arguments. The only way to change a feeling is to replace it with another feeling. We should be able to replace an unpleasant emotion such as fear, anger, guilt, or sadness with love, forgiveness, and joy.

c) *Modifying our reaction to others.* Sympathy means to appreciate the other person's emotion. Empathy means to actually *feel* the same as the other person. Every individual has his or her own perceptual pattern. Our points of view are different because our perceptions are different. Empathy is our skill to feel close to others and understand them. It allows us to recognize the other person as different rather than difficult. We have two levels of existence, head-centred judgment and heart-centred affiliation. Once we learn the skill of shifting from head to heart, we have learned the art of self-healing through altruistic love and the capacity to forgive.

d) *Motivation* depends on how our belief system is and how we choose to delay our gratification. We must learn to strike a balance between impulse and restraint, id and ego. Our emotion at the moment is the result of what we are able to choose and what we are able to avoid in our experience of the moment. We should be able to enter a state of flow at least in some of our daily activities. The state of flow refers to forgetting ourselves while doing something we like to do.

e) *Managing our relationships.* This is our social intelligence, how we give and receive energy to and from our spouse, family, co-workers, and society at large. In our vertical relationship, we need to use optimal energy in managing our energy by understanding our mind-body dialogue in relation to our emotions, and transcend our impulses in order to control situations through a spiritual and altruistic perspective. One key aspect in modern life is how we relate to money. Is someone spending more than half of his or her waking time in thinking and planning about money and material possessions? If so, logically the person may be successful, but biologically a misfit.

Healing means making ourselves whole. This requires the 'external pharmacy' of doctor-prescribed drugs (if it's unavoidable) and 'internal pharmacy' of managing our emotions in addition to the matter- and motion-dynamics of modern life. Mindfulness of the present moment and self-regulation of our body in relation to each emotion are two key factors in managing our emotions. Altruism (*sevā*, in Sanskrit) is a powerful antidote to anger, the most powerful negative emotion. Altruism starts with non-judgmental heart-centred living, which must eventually become our natural way of life. Let us begin the practice rightaway.

18

Prisoner of One's Own Habits

ANONYMOUS*

The beginning was a disturbed childhood, a habit of drinking and no good purpose in life. At eighteen I landed in jail on a charge of petty theft, which started the vicious circle of theft for easy money and a good time, arrest, trial, prison sentence, hate for society, release, and again theft and thoughts of murder for revenge.

Reversing the Vicious Circle

After eight months I began to feel the effects of imprisonment. Luckily, sickness came—insomnia, consti-

---

* This is an ex-convict's article which appeared in a Yoga Journal published in Belgium—*Ed*.

pation and headache, and a daily routine of visiting sick bay. Drugs were given without much relief and even more symptoms appeared. I began to think it was due to the prison food, so I obtained a book on dietetics.

One time I accidentally visited the prison butchery and received a terrible shock. Hanging upside down was half an animal, frozen nine years earlier. From then on I stopped eating meat. This was indeed difficult to manage inside a prison. While others were trying to get alcohol and medicine, I was trying to obtain fresh and healthy food.

Slowly I began to feel better, which assured me that I was moving on the right path. Then I discovered yoga and began practising from a book. It was the only physical exercise possible in the confines of a cell. As I performed different asanas I felt a transformation taking place, not only outwardly but also inwardly. I suddenly realized that my life had been a succession of mistakes and that hate was a much heavier burden for myself than it was for those who were the object of it.

Breaking Out of Negative Habits

I was still drinking alcohol and smoking nearly three packets of cigarettes a day. I learned that this was weakening my heart and destroying my lungs. It was the reason I was coughing and spitting.

Over one week I decided not to smoke during my walking hour and it was quite an ordeal. Progressively I reduced the number of cigarettes daily. I thought finally, 'I will get rid of this smoking habit,' and repeated this sentence again and again. Then I began breathing more deeply and with awareness for the first time. Finally I exchanged my cigarette provision for sweets. However, this need slowly disappeared and, with my success in giving up smoking, I decided to win over my alcohol habit also. That was another victory. Gradually I got rid of many unhealthy habits and this improved all levels of my being—physical, mental, emotional and psychic.

Reforming the Inner Man

Here I was, however, still a slave of my negative thoughts, so I consciously decided to transform my thinking and my mind. Now I understand that the first steps of transformation started with taking responsibility for my own health and habits. My conscious efforts started with one of the most destructive emotions in man—hate. Where there was hate, there would be love; where there was selfishness, there would be generosity; etc. I wrote these maxims down and repeated them like a sankalpa every day.

I realized then that I was the only one responsible for my evil tendencies. No matter what injustice I felt in this world, I decided to forget all ideas of revenge. It felt good to live without hate but in peace with all. Even my cell seemed larger and more pleasant. A new life was blooming before me—one of love for others and nature, for everything, in fact, that made up our existence. The metamorphosis resulted in a new and happy man with many inspiring friends made through continued study of health, yoga and dietetics. This revealed to me that the outer world changes as one's inner world evolves.

A Life Sentence of Freedom

After five years of jail, a warder came to my cell and told me, 'You are free.' I smiled. *I was already free*—free of the ideas which bound me more than anything else. The reason I am relating this today, is for anybody suffering in similar circumstances; living with hate; or thinking it's too late to change. It is possible to change the world—that is, our view of the world—to a beautiful and positive one. You can expand your health, awareness and happiness with fresh, nourishing food, yogic disciplines, and a balanced life-style.

This is not the first time that yoga and a higher life have been discovered inside prison walls. Being 'inside' is a time when one can reflect on one's life, to think, to meditate, to make decisions to change, or to continue the downward spiral of self-destruction. In the words of Tagore:

> I was asleep and dreaming
> That life was only joy.
> I woke up and saw
> That life was all service.
> I served and saw
> That service was pure joy.

19

"Look at the Ocean"

SWAMI TYAGANANDA

Look at the "ocean" and not at the "wave".... Although we appear as little waves, the whole ocean is at our back, and we are one with it. No wave can exist of itself. This whole universe is my body; all health, all happiness is mine, because all is in the universe. Say, "I am the universe."

Swami Vivekananda, CW 7: 7, 8: 49

Health and happiness always go together. If I am not happy, it means something is wrong with my health. The reverse is also true. If I am not healthy, I cannot really be happy.

What is said above will not make sense if our understanding of both health and happiness is superficial. Health is something more than just the well-being of the body. It means the well-being of the mind as well. And something more also—the well-being of the spiritual dimension of our personality.[1]

Similarly, happiness is something more than the pleasant feeling we get from the fulfilment of our desires. At best, this kind of feeling is only a short-lived shadow of *true* happiness, which is a deep-rooted, never-ceasing experience of joy born of the awareness of our complete well-being, our limitlessness and infinitude. Vedanta recognized this truth about happiness several thousand years ago. The Chāndogya Upaniṣad 7.23.1 says: 'The infinite is bliss. There is no bliss in anything finite. Only the infinite is blissful.'[2]

If health and happiness are interrelated and interdependent and if they can be found only in the infinite, then we know what we must do to be healthy and happy. We must become infinite. Our present limitedness is self-evident. I have my own body, different from your body and different from all the other bodies in the world: my body is limited. I have my own mind, different from your mind and different from all the other minds in the world: my mind is limited. And for those amongst us who figure that we have (we are?) a third something, different from both body and mind—called the soul or spirit or Ātman (self)—well, I have my own Ātman, different from yours and different from all the other Ātmans in the world: my Ātman is limited. We don't generally question the truth of this threefold limitedness because it is so obvious.

Vedanta says that what is obvious need not always represent the truth. The very obviousness of a thing or a phenomenon could be an obstacle preventing us from looking more deeply. What is it that we find by looking deeply into our 'obvious' limitedness? Simply this: our limitedness is a myth, a lie we keep telling ourselves. Every one of us is individually the infinite being. Furthermore, our very nature is joyful. Being happy is our natural state.

The reason we don't *feel* ourselves to be infinite and ever-happy is that we are not really and fully healthy. Something is wrong with us. We are not being our true selves. We are, as it were, standing outside of ourselves. To be healthy is to be *svastha,* 'standing on my own self.' *Svastha* is a word frequently used in India. 'Are you *svastha*?' they ask here—meaning, 'Are you well, are you happy?'[3]

Someone might say, okay, I accept the possibility that I am really the infinite being. Can Vedanta tell me, one, why I feel I am limited and, two, how I can become my original infinite self? Vedanta teachers answer these questions in their usual direct manner. They might say something like this. I feel I am limited for the same reason as why I feel the sun rises in the east and sets in the west. The sunrise and the sunset are matters of my daily experience; I cannot deny them. But when I learn the truth I won't be able to deny that the sun never rises and never sets—it's the earth that rotates and creates the illusion of the sun's movement. Similarly, my limitedness is a matter of my daily experience; I cannot deny it. But when I learn the truth I won't be able to deny that my limitedness was only an illusion, a bad dream, a silly figment of imagination.

The second question—how can I become my original infinite self?—is automatically answered by ' . . . when I learn the truth.' But let's get our language straight. At present I feel I'm limited; that's fine. No problem there. The question is, have I *really* become limited? If I have become limited, then simply 'knowing' I am infinite won't make me infinite.[4] It's like this: if the sun has *really* started rising and setting, then merely 'knowing' that the sun neither rises nor sets won't make it stop its movement. So we have this other possibility: ignorance or forgetfulness. I have somehow forgotten my true nature and am mistakenly seeing myself as a limited creature. Since it's only a mistake, I haven't *really* become limited but am only behaving like a limited being. So 'knowing' I am infinite is enough to rectify the error. I am always my infinite self. It's just that I have forgotten it—and now need to know the truth.

Someone comes and tells me, or I read in some Vedanta book: 'You are the infinite being. Don't delude yourself ever with the idea that you are a limited creature. You are ever-free, ever-perfect, birthless and deathless, blessed and blissful.' Ah, I say, *now* I know the truth, and for a moment or two I feel great. But only for a moment or two. Soon enough it's time for dinner or a neighbour calls to borrow the lawn mower or I remember I've to do the dishes —and the momentary knowledge of my unlimitedness vanishes into thin air and I become the same old limited insect again.

So what good is this knowledge? Vedanta teachers answer this by saying, look, your knowledge is only indirect (*parokṣa*). It's good but not enough. What you need is to transform your indirect knowledge into direct (*aparokṣa*) knowledge or experience. Now you know that milk is white and nutritious. But until you drink milk, it cannot nourish you. If your knowledge is to 'nourish' you, you must 'drink' it.[5]

To See Is to Be

How can I 'drink' the knowledge of my infinite nature? There are several ways to do this. One way is the look-at-the-ocean method taught by Swami Vivekananda. It is based on the principle: 'To see is to be.' Swamiji said,

> Change the subject and the object is bound to change. Purify yourself and the world is bound to be purified. This one thing requires to be taught now more than ever before. . . . The world will change if we change; if we are pure the world will become pure. The question is why I should see evil in others. I cannot *see* evil unless I *be* evil.[6]

Using this insight in the present context, I must realize I would not have been able to *see* limitedness all around me if I had not made my own self limited. *Change the subject and the object is bound to change,* Swamiji says. So I must break all limiting barriers and start seeing myself as infinite.

It's not too difficult if we really put our mind to it. After all, seeing myself as I truly am should be the easiest thing in the world. It's easy to be truthful, it is very difficult to be a consistent lier. Swamiji asks us to focus on the truth when he says: 'Look at the ocean and not at the wave'[7] — meaning, look at your true self, the infinite, the whole, the ever-lasting; stop getting devoured by the limited, the part, the ever-vanishing.

How can we look at the ocean and not see the wave? That would be impossible unless we have some way of making the waves disappear. Such a way exists. The first thing is to recognize that the wave is not different from the vast, limitless expanse of water we call the ocean; it's, after all, a part of the ocean. The second thing is to recognize that a wave is at the same time different from the ocean. We never mistake the one for the other, do we? A wave has an identity of its own—it's got a recognizable form. The third thing is to recognize that the form of the wave is temporary. The wave lasts only so long as its form lasts. The wave ceases to be a wave the moment its form subsides. The fourth thing is to recognize that once the form vanishes, we cannot distinguish the wave anymore from the vast expanse of water, because the wave itself is essentially only water. In this way we look deeply at the ocean and see just the ocean, not the waves.

The next time we are on the beach we might try to practise the above 'four recognitions.' If we are lucky—and there is no reason why we shouldn't be—we'll be able to make the waves disappear from our consciousness. Some day we'll discover we are bobbing up and down, being pushed here and there, now in one form, now in another, in the limitless ocean of existence.[8] The Absolute, or God, is that infinite ocean, while you and I and suns and stars and everything else are waves in that ocean.[9] What makes us different from the Absolute and from one another? Only the form.[10] Once the fences separating me from others are broken, what remains is only the infinite ocean, call it the Absolute, or God—or, ah well, me in my true nature. The 'four recognitions' can make the waves disappear from this cosmic ocean, leaving behind only one unchanging, unlimited, undying reality.

To help us grasp this idea, Swamiji begins by telling us not of one ocean but three! Corresponding to the three so-called parts of our personality—body, mind, and

Ātman—we have three oceans: the ocean of matter, the ocean of ideas, and the ocean of consciousness.

The Ocean of Matter

Those with a little scientific background have no difficulty in understanding that there are no *physical* boundaries separating one thing from another. Colour, density, composition, and configuration may vary between things, but it's all one continuous, unbroken whole as far as matter is concerned. Materially speaking, there is no intrinsic difference between a human body, a potato, and a meteorite. The basic building blocks for all these are same. This is perhaps what ' . . . dust thou art, and unto dust shalt thou return' really means.[11]

All around us and within us is one big ocean of matter. As water flows freely from one point to another in the ocean, here too in the ocean of matter there is a free flow of matter. What this means is that nothing remains unchanged for an indefinite period. A thing should no more be seen as an object; it's only a form. At the microscopic level matter is continuously being thrown out and new matter being absorbed into forms that appear as 'things' to our eyes. Vivekananda said:

> No man was ever born who could stop his body one moment from changing. Body is the name of a series of changes. 'As in a river the masses of water are changing before you every moment, and new masses are coming, yet taking similar form, so is it with this body.'[12]

Here's one account of the process described by a contemporary researcher:

The river is constantly being changed by new water rushing in. The same holds true for the body. All of us are much more like a river than anything frozen in time and space.

If you could see your body as it really is, you would never see it the same way twice. Ninety-eight percent of the atoms in your body were not there a year ago. The skeleton that seems so solid was not there three months ago. The configuration of the bone cells remains somewhat constant, but atoms of all kinds pass freely back and forth through the cell walls, and by that means you acquire a new skeleton every three months.

The skin is new every month. You have a new stomach lining every four days, with the actual surface cells that contact food being renewed every five minutes. The cells in the liver turn over very slowly, but new atoms still flow through them, like water in a river course, making a new liver every six weeks. Even within the brain, whose cells are not replaced once they die, the content of carbon, nitrogen, oxygen, and so on is totally different today from a year ago.

It is as if you lived in a building whose bricks were systematically taken out and replaced every year. If you keep the same blueprint, then it will still look like the same building. But it won't be the same in actuality. The human body also stands there looking much the same from day to day, but through the process of respiration, digestion, elimination, and so forth, it is constantly and ever in exchange with the rest of the world.[13]

Through this 'exchange with the rest of the world' we can see, if we look deeply enough, the entire world within our body.

Here is an apple. We know it didn't drop from the heavens. It grew on an apple tree which began its life's journey in the form of a tiny seed. Water, manure, sunshine have all contributed towards transforming that seed into a tree. Without these there would have been no tree and hence no apple. When we see an apple, we can see in it sunshine, water-bearing clouds, organic plant-food, even the labour of the person who picked the fruit and transported it to the market.

When I eat an apple, all these 'non-apple elements' which make up the apple (an expression Zen Master Thích Nhat Hanh is fond of using) go *in* my body and, a few hours later, some of them become a part of my body; the rest are eliminated and recycled. Thus clouds, sunshine and the rest are now all ingredients of my physical self. Particles of matter from the moon and Mars are probably in the stretch of the garden I can see from my window—and, who knows, before long they might be a part of my own body.[14]

You and I are 'born' inside a huge ocean of matter, with whirling, swirling particles that flow freely through apparently unchanging forms.[15] If I can make these 'form'-waves disappear from the ocean—and we have seen the 'four recognitions' which can help us do that—several benefits come to me.

First and foremost comes a new insight into the meaning of death. We realize that death is not destruction but a mere disappearance of the wave—the 'form' of the body—into the ocean of matter. It is possible to speak of even physical immortality, because the ocean remains—and I am the ocean. It's only the forms that come and go. Listen to what Vivekananda says:

> There can be no physical death for us and no material death when we see that all is one. All bodies are mine; so even body is eternal, because the tree, the animal, the sun, the moon, the universe itself is my body; then how can it die? . . . If a hair falls out, we do not think we die; so if one body dies, it is but a hair falling.[16]

When I look at the ocean and see it even within the waves, I begin to understand what being birthless and deathless means. Swamiji says:

> He alone lives whose life is in the whole universe ['the ocean'], and the more we concentrate our lives on limited things ['waves'], the faster we go towards death. . . . The fear of death can be conquered when man realizes . . . 'I am in everything, in everybody, I am in all lives, I am the universe,' then alone comes the state of fearlessness.[17]

Can the ocean become jealous of its waves? Will it love some waves more than it does others? No, this sounds crazy. When we feel one with the ocean of matter, we automatically develop the quality of same-sightedness. Hatred, jealousy, envy become meaningless, because I am then able to see myself in other bodies, and other bodies within my body. All distinctions based on colour, race, caste and religion seem silly when we realize that physically we are not distinct at all. There is constant exchange of matter between, say, a black person and a white person, an upper-caste person and a lower-caste person, a Jew and an Arab. Where does this leave all the talk of white supremacy, racial purity, caste superiority, and religious exclusiveness?

Speaking of exchange of matter, we are awakened to the question of food. We cannot see with the naked eye the body's exchange of matter with the rest of the world. But when we think of food we understand the process readily. If the essence of what I eat is going to *be* a component of my body, I become careful about what I eat. I wouldn't like people throwing junk into my room, so how I can allow my own self to throw junk food in my body? Since the body's food is going to *be* the body, I will want to have healthy food for a healthy body. Thus diet-consciousness comes naturally to one who sees the ocean of matter.

My body can get healthy food and pure water and my lungs can get clean air only if these are available. Thus the ocean-consciousness makes me aware of environmental and ecological issues. This awareness can come even without the ocean-idea, but it acquires special urgency and greater intensity when I see myself helplessly exchanging matter every moment with the polluted environment around me. I *must* do something, I feel, and the planet Earth gets one more defender committed to prevent the collective self-destruction of humanity.

We have seen that the-ocean-of-matter awareness minimizes our fear of death; helps in the cultivation of the virtue of same-sightedness; prevents the rise of negative qualities such as jealousy, envy, hatred; pushes us to develop healthy food habits; and makes us live in an environment-friendly manner.

All of these benefits get strengthened and some more are added to the list when we become aware of yet another ocean—the ocean of ideas.

The Ocean of Ideas

The physicalness of the body and of the things we see around us is unquestionable. But what about the mind? It can neither be seen nor touched nor smelled nor tasted nor heard. But we know it's there. In Western thought the mind is usually considered nonmaterial and is sometimes used synonymously with the word 'soul'. In India, however, the idea of mind being nonmaterial was rejected thousands of years ago. The Vedic sages were bold and brave thinkers. Seeing that the mind—like any material object—is subject to change and periodic disappearance (as in deep sleep), they said the mind too is material. It is made up of fine or subtle (*sūkṣma*) matter.

Every one of us has a mind but none of these minds is an isolated something. The sages in ancient India discovered that

> each mind is connected with every other mind. And each mind, wherever it is located, is in actual communication with the whole world.[18]

How did they find this out? Through the phenomenon called thought-transference. Swamiji explains:

> A man here is thinking something, and that thought is manifested in somebody else, in some other place. With preparations —not by chance—a man wants to send a thought to another mind at a distance, and this other mind knows that a thought is coming, and he receives it exactly as it is sent out. Distance makes no difference. The thought goes and reaches the other man, and he understands it.
>
> If your mind were an isolated something here, and my mind were an isolated something there, and there were no connection between the two, how would it be possible for my thought to reach you?
>
> In the ordinary cases [such as when I *tell* you my thoughts], it is not my thought that is reaching you direct; but my thought has got to be dissolved into ethereal vibrations ['sound waves'] and those ethereal vibrations go into your brain [via the ear and the auditory nerve], and they have to be resolved again into your own thoughts. Here is a dissolution of thought, and there is a resolution of thought. It is a roundabout process.

But in telepathy, there is no such thing; it is direct. This shows that there is a continuity of mind, as the yogis call it. The mind is universal. Your mind, my mind, all these little minds, are fragments of that universal mind, little waves in the ocean; and on account of this continuity, we can convey our thoughts directly to one another.[19]

The ocean of matter is another name for the universal body. Since the bodies, living and nonliving, are all gross (*sthūla*) and accessible to the sense-organs, the ocean of matter is really the ocean of *gross* matter. When we deal with the mind, we are dealing with subtle matter. The universal mind, therefore, is the ocean of *subtle* matter—and, for convenience, we'll call it the ocean of ideas.[20]

Applying the 'four recognitions' it is possible to look at this ocean of ideas and ignore the waves, *including* the wave of my own mind. If my own mind disappears, won't I lose my identity, my individuality? No, says Vedanta.

There is no individuality except in the Infinite ['the ocean']. That is the only condition which does not change. Everything else ['waves'] is in a constant state of flux.[21]

A wave's true identity is the water, not the wave-form. When a wave subsides, it does lose something, it is true; what it loses is the wave-form—and that is good, because the form was a hurdle, a limiting barrier, preventing the wave from realizing its oneness with the ocean. A wave without the wave-form is nothing but the ocean. So when I'm able to pierce through my mind-form, I'll realize my oneness with the ocean of ideas. *That* is my true identity in the mental world.

What are the special benefits we get by looking at the ocean of ideas? First off, all wave-forms, including the form of my mind, vanish or become inconsequential. The little 'I' of the wave is forgotten and, as Vivekananda said, 'forgetting the little "I" is a sign of healthy and pure mind.'[22] In little children this happens spontaneously but, ironically, as they grow bigger their 'I' gets smaller and they invite all the maladies we adults are suffering from now.

The ocean-consciousness can produce in me a strong detachment from my own obsessions and pet notions, worries and anxieties, joys and sorrows. I begin to sense that these are not really my own any more than they are of others'. If I attach myself to them, I limit myself and suffer; instead I can 'look at the ocean' and remain detached, happy, and free from most mental illnesses.

Another benefit is that we are able to open ourselves to other minds instead of remaining cocooned within our own. Real communication and education are possible only when our ears and minds are open, and not just the mouths. Such a lot can be learnt from the thoughts and ideas freely floating in this ocean if we only know how to open the gates of our mind!

From the spiritual standpoint, the world of ideas is 'purer' and 'higher' than the world of gross matter. To be identified with the ocean of ideas is, therefore, a more fulfilling, soothing, uplifting experience than to be identified with the relatively more turbulent and turbid ocean of gross matter. Vivekananda's disciple Sister Nivedita once confided that she had achieved a breakthrough: whenever she dealt with a person she had begun to feel she was dealing with 'a mind.' The body was so secondary and incidental that it got no attention.

How much of fear and anxiety, jealousy and envy are produced by this thing called 'ownership'! People are afraid of losing the things they own, apprehensive that their things may be stolen, anxious to own new things, and envious of those who have more than they do. This is true not only with regard to material things but also—perhaps more—with regard to ideas. The term 'intellectual property' would have been incomprehensible to the Vedic sages, who freely shared their discoveries without even bothering to tag them with their own names. They knew the utter stupidity of waves claiming ownership of the water enclosed in their soon-to-vanish forms.

If the ocean of gross matter is connected with the well-being of our gross body, then the ocean of subtle matter (we have called it 'the ocean of ideas') is connected with the well-being of our subtle body, or mind. But these two oceans are themselves connected to one another, making them jointly responsible for the well-being of our body-mind. It is possible to view these two oceans of matter, gross and subtle, as just one ocean.

The Ocean of Life

The Vedic sages resolved the whole universe into one material, which they called Ākāśa. To continue in Swamiji's words:

> Everything that we see around us, feel, touch, taste, is simply a differentiated manifestation of this Akasha. It is all-pervading, fine. All that we call solids, liquids, or gases, figures, forms, or bodies, the earth, sun, moon, and stars—everything is composed of this Akasha.

What force is it which acts upon this Akasha and manu-
factures this universe out of it? Along with Akasha exists
universal power; all that is power in the universe, manifesting as
force or attraction—nay, even as thought—is but a different
manifestation of that one power which the Hindus call Prana.
This Prana, acting on Akasha, is creating the whole of this
universe.[23]

Since the power that activates—brings to life, so to
say—the ocean of matter, producing waves both subtle and
gross, is Prāṇa ('life-energy'), it is considered the basic principle of life. So long as Prāṇa is active, there is life; when
Prāṇa goes to sleep, as it were, life ceases to be. So it is
right to re-name the oceans of gross and subtle matter as
the one ocean of life.[24]

The combining of the two oceans into one implies
that the two are interdependent and interconnected. The
benefits we acquire by identifying with any one of the two
oceans, get reinforced and strengthened by identifying with
the other also. Furthermore, the two act and react upon one
another. This naturally means that the 'waves' in the two
oceans also act and react upon one another. It's easy to
understand now why body and mind are interconnected.
Swamiji describes what this leads to in effect:

If we believe that the mind is simply a finer part of the body,
and that mind acts upon the body, then it stands to reason that
the body must react upon the mind. If the body is sick, the mind
becomes sick also. If the body is healthy, the mind remains
healthy and strong. When one is angry, the mind becomes disturbed. And when the mind is disturbed, the body also becomes
disturbed.[25]

The influence of body on mind, and vice versa, are
seldom equal. In most people the mind is greatly under the

control of the body; in them, the changes in the mind hardly affect the body. Such people, Swamiji says, are 'very little removed from the animals.'[26] But there are others with a developed and refined mind which exercises control over the body; in them, because of greater sensitivity, the changes in the mind affect the body considerably, but the mind is usually strong enough to remain relatively unaffected by physical changes or disorders.

We have had a look at two oceans, the ocean of matter and the ocean of ideas. We have also seen how the two are interconnected and can be considered as just one ocean, the ocean of life. What I call my body is a mere wave in the ocean of matter; what I call my mind is another wave in the ocean of ideas. Or, if we combine the two, for both are made of matter, what I call my body-mind is just a wave in the ocean of life.

As a wave, every moment I am changing. Every moment material is being added to me and every moment material is being thrown off by me. And yet I know I am the same person, not only moment after moment, but also day after day, year after year. In the midst of this constant change in both body and mind, what is it that makes me feel I am the same person? Swamiji answers:

> In spite of this continuous change in the body, and in spite of this continuous change in the mind, there is in us something that is unchangeable, which makes our ideas of things appear unchangeable. When rays of light coming from different quarters fall upon a screen, or a wall, or upon something that is not changeable, then and then alone it is possible for them to form a unity, then and then alone it is possible for them to form one complete whole. Where is this unity in the human organs, falling upon which, as it were, the various ideas will come to unity

and become one complete whole? This certainly cannot be the mind itself, seeing that it also changes.

Therefore there must be something which is neither the body nor the mind, something which changes not, something permanent, upon which all our ideas, our sensations fall to form a unity and a complete whole; and this is the real soul, the Atman.

And seeing that everything material, whether you call it fine matter, or mind, must be changeful; seeing that what you call gross matter, the external world, must also be changeful in comparison to that—this unchangeable something cannot be of material substance; therefore it is spiritual, that is to say, it is not matter—it is indestructible, unchangeable.[27]

This brings us to the third ocean, corresponding to the third aspect of our personality.

The Ocean of Consciousness

Although the ocean of consciousness is the third ocean we are being told to look at, there are not really three oceans. There is only one. The two oceans we have seen earlier, the ocean of matter and the ocean of ideas (or, taken together, the ocean of life), are only parts of the ocean of consciousness.[28] And these are so insignificant and trivial parts of it that they may as well be considered two tiny waves of gross and subtle matter (or one tiny wave of life) in the infinite, shoreless ocean of consciousness.[29] This gives us a faint idea of how awfully limited we have made ourselves, because a small wave of matter appears to us at present to be as large as an ocean.

The 'Puruṣa-Sūkta' in the Ṛg-Veda makes it perfectly clear that only a tiny fraction of the Absolute comes into

being as the world, physical and mental; most of the
Absolute remains ever-transcendent.[30] But expressing it
even this way can be misleading, for it creates the impres-
sion of there being two entities, the transcendent Absolute
and its immanent portion manifesting as the physical world
('the ocean of matter') and the mental world ('the ocean of
ideas'). There is no such division really. Swamiji says:

> There are no such realities as a physical world, a mental world,
> a spiritual world. *Whatever is, is one.* Let us say, it is a sort of
> tapering existence; the thickest part is here, it tapers and be-
> comes finer and finer. The finest is what we call spirit; the
> grossest, the body. And just as it is here in microcosm, it is
> exactly the same in the macrocosm. The universe of ours is
> exactly like that; it is the gross external thickness, and it tapers
> into something finer and finer until it becomes God.[31]

If we had some way of returning gross matter to its
origin or cause, we shall see that it just vanishes, leaving
only the subtle matter behind; and if we had some way of
returning this subtle matter to *its* origin, we shall see that
it also vanishes, leaving only the spirit behind.

This 'returning process' in our individual lives takes
the form of what is called self-purification. When my body
becomes totally pure, it will vanish. Vanish? Not literally,
but figuratively. That means I'll live as if my body were not
there. My body won't make its presence felt, it won't assert
its demands, I won't feel its weight. It'll become a kind of
shadow, existing but unimportant.

The same thing will happen to my mind. When my
mind will becomes totally pure, it too will vanish, meaning
it'll cease bossing over me, it won't drag me here and
there, I won't feel myself trapped in it. This process of self-

purification will reveal to us what Swamiji calls 'finer and finer' dimensions of our being until we reach the 'finest'— the spirit or God, or 'the ocean of consciousness.'[32] To realize my oneness with this infinite ocean of consciousness is, according to Vedanta, to be in a state of perfect health and joy.

As a result of some mysterious quirk, this normally unchanging, undisturbed ocean seems to have produced a 'wave' of its own, triggering a chain reaction which produces the oceans of gross and subtle matter with their zillions of waves. What began basically as spiritual sickness has ended up producing physical and mental sicknesses of all kinds. Not for nothing does Vedanta say that there is a spiritual solution to every problem. Since the basic problem is spiritual, the best solution cannot but be spiritual.

What We Waves Must Do Now

Having seen—so far only theoretically—the three oceans and their integration into just one, we must come to terms with the fact that each one of us is now only a wave. That at least is what our present experience is.

To erase our false wave-identity and regain our true ocean-identity we must, of course, practise the 'four recognitions' at all times and in all situations. This is clearly asking for the moon. So to begin with, it is good to 'look at the ocean' at least for a few minutes at fixed hours.

Immediately after waking in the morning and before hitting the sack at night are two best times to look at the ocean. Creative imagination can be an asset if employed to produce useful, authentic images. Sri Ramakrishna's guru

Totapuri offered the following image when he instructed his disciple about the nature of the Absolute:

> [The Absolute] is like an infinite ocean—water everywhere, to the right, left, above, and below. Water enveloped in water. It is the Water of the Great Cause, motionless. Waves spring up when It becomes active. Its activities are creation, preservation, and destruction.[33]

Vivekananda once gave the following subject for meditation which can be used by any of us:

> Above, it is full of me; below, it is full of me; in the middle, it is full of me. I am in all beings, and all beings are in me. Om Tat Sat, I am It. I am existence above mind. I am the one Spirit of the universe. I am neither pleasure nor pain.
>
> The body drinks, eats, and so on. I am not the body. I am not the mind. . . . I am Existence, Knowledge, Bliss.
>
> I am the essence and nectar of knowledge. Through eternity I change not. I am calm, resplendent, and unchanging.[34]

Chanting of certain Upaniṣadic texts might help us to hold on to the ocean-image. For instance the following:

> The Supreme light [of consciousness] which shines as the substratum of the liquid element—I am that Supreme Light. I am that supreme light of Brahman which shines as the inmost essence of all that exists. I am the infinite Brahman ['the ocean of consciousness'] even when I am experiencing myself as a limited self ['wave'] due to ignorance. Now I know that I am really Brahman and that is my true nature. I offer my false, limited self into the fire of Brahman, my true, infinite Self. May this oblation be well made.[35]
>
> The Self ['the ocean of consciousness'], indeed, is below. The Self is above. The Self is behind. The Self is in front. The Self is to the south. The Self is to the north. The Self, indeed, is all this.[36]

Here, though the Self refers to our spiritual self, or Ātman, the passage is equally relevant to our so-called physical self (body) and mental self (mind), and can be effectively employed to look at the ocean of matter and the ocean of ideas also.

In addition to our fixed-hour practice, we can try to 'look at the ocean' throughout the day whenever we sense our wave-identity overwhelming us. It doesn't really take more than ten or fifteen seconds, perhaps even less, to have a quick look at the ocean and return to the job on hand. Not only will this restore our peace and joy, it will also improve the quality of our work. We'll know exactly the right way to do right things at the right time.

If we persist with the look-at-the-ocean practice, within a few weeks we shall discover a new world around us and we ourselves too shall become 'new'. Our wave-identity is unlikely to vanish immediately (after all, we have built it up over an enormously long period), but the walls separating us from the rest of the world won't be absolutely uncrossable. To the extent the ocean-consciousness becomes stronger, the wave-consciousness would become weaker.

We have already seen the benefits of looking at the ocean of matter and the ocean of ideas. So it is sufficient to say here that our look-at-the-ocean practice would alter our life-style in such a way as to produce good physical health and strong mental health, creating ideal conditions to cultivate spiritual health. This is not to say there would be no physical illnesses or mental upsets, but these would be rare occurrences and, even when they do occur, they won't throw us off balance.

The ocean-awareness makes us a witness, so we might be able to say, 'I am the witness. I look on. When health comes I am the witness. When disease comes I am the witness.'[37] Even when the so-called death comes, I can be the witness. The Sanskrit word for body is *śarīra,* literally 'that which wears away or disintegrates.'[38] So when the time comes for body's inevitable coming-apart, I can look at it calmly. The goal is not to perpetuate our illusory wave-identity, but to realize its emptiness and return to our true ocean-identity.

The loss of the ocean-identity was due to sickness produced by the virus of 'ignorance' (*avidyā*). Its immediate effect was self-forgetfulness, leading to not only my being a fragile, vulnerable, insecure, mortal creature but also seeing around me a world that is disconnected, sometimes hostile, often meaningless, and always unfulfilling.

The effort to regain the ocean-identity builds bridges where there seemed none, produces love that unites hearts and serves the needy, brings meaning into life and makes it progressively more fulfilling. When I become reestablished in the ocean-consciousness, that is to say, when I *experience* the truth 'I am the ocean,' I shall be free from spiritual sickness, which is the root cause of all sicknesses physical and mental.

When I see myself in all beings and all beings in me, I'll attain health which can never be lost and happiness which can never be clouded. Many waves have already become one with the ocean and attained to complete well-being, absolute freedom, unceasing joy, and true immortality. Fellow waves! What are *we* waiting for?

NOTES & REFERENCES

1. On this basis it is possible to study health in its threefold aspects: physical health, mental health, and spiritual health.

2. यो वै भूमा तत् सुखं, नाल्पे सुखं अस्ति, भूमैव सुखम् ।

3. *The Complete Works of Swami Vivekananda,* 8 vols. (Calcutta: Advaita Ashrama, 1972–77), 7: 82 (hereafter cited as CW, followed by volume and page numbers). See also CW 4: 228.

4. If I have *really* become limited, then it only means my unlimitedness was an illusion. A truly infinite thing can never become finite. Infinity cannot be divided.

5. Sri Ramakrishna often used this illustration to show the difference between the two kinds of knowledge. See *The Gospel of Sri Ramakrishna,* trans. Swami Nikhilananda (Madras: Sri Ramakrishna Math, 1980), 344, 368, 404, 417, 478, 829, 836 (hereafter cited as *Gospel*).

6. CW 1: 426.

7. CW 7: 7.

8. Shortly after meeting Sri Ramakrishna, Swamiji had through the grace of his Guru a mystic vision of this limitless ocean of existence and, for a few days after that, everything appeared to him to be made of 'one stuff.' 'Looking at the ocean' became natural to him a little later. See His Eastern and Western Disciples, *The Life of Swami Vivekananda,* 2 vols. (Calcutta: Advaita Ashrama, 1979), 1: 96–97.

9. See CW 3: 188, 241.

10. See CW 2: 136.

11. Genesis 3: 19.

12. CW 1: 142. Swamiji is here partly paraphrasing the *Bhāgavata,* 11.22.44—

सोऽयं दीपोऽर्चिषां यद्वत् स्रोतसां तदिदं जलम् ।
सोऽयं पुमानिति नृणां मृषा गीर्धीर्मृषायुषाम् ॥

13. Deepak Chopra, *Quantum Healing: "Exploring the Frontiers of Mind/Body Medicine* (Bantam Books, 1990), 48–49.

14. See also CW 1: 14.
15. See CW 3: 404.
16. CW 7: 93–94
17. CW 2: 80–81.
18. CW 2: 13.
19. CW 2: 13.
20. See CW 3: 241.
21. CW 2: 80.
22. CW 6: 119.
23. CW 2: 263–64.
24. By 'life' is meant here that which is inseparable from its counter-part, 'death'.
25. CW 1: 132.
26. Ibid.
27. CW 3: 404–5.
28. 'Life-energy' or just 'life' (*prāṇa*) and consciousness (*caitanya*) seem to us intertwined, even identical. But the two are quite different. For an insightful study on this subject, see Swami Shraddha-nanda's *Seeing God Everywhere: 'A Practical Guide to Spiritual Living,'* ed. Pravrajika Vrajaprana (Hollywood: Vedanta Press, 1996), 122–28.
29. Consciousness shows through 'matter' because 'matter' is only a wave in the ocean of consciousness. That is why body and mind appear 'conscious'.
30. *Ṛg-Veda,* 10.90.3—

पादोऽस्य विश्वा भूतानि त्रिपादस्यामृतं दिवि ।

See also *Gītā,* 10.42—

विष्टभ्याहमिदं कृत्स्नमेकांशेन स्थितो जगत् ।

31. CW 2: 16.
32. Sri Ramakrishna once described what is almost certainly one of his many visions of 'the ocean of consciousness.' In the Divine Mother's temple at Dakshineswar he saw the deity, the altar, the pūjā ves-sels and everything including himself made of pure consciousness.

33. *Gospel*, 358.

34. CW 6: 91–92.

35. *Mahānārāyaṇa Upaniṣad*, 1.67--

> आर्द्रं ज्वलति ज्योतिरहमस्मि । ज्योतिर्ज्वलति ब्रह्माहमस्मि । योऽहमस्मि
> ब्रह्माहमस्मि । अहमस्मि ब्रह्माहमस्मि । अहमेवाहं मां जुहोमि स्वाहा ॥

36. *Chāndogya Upaniṣad*, 7.25.2—

> आत्मैव-अधस्ताद्, आत्मोपरिष्टाद्, आत्मा पश्चाद्, आत्मा पुरस्ताद्, आत्मा
> दक्षिणत, आत्मोत्तरत, आत्मैव-इदं सर्वम् इति ।

37. CW 6: 91.

38. शीर्यते इति शरीरम् ।

Contributors

SWAMI GAUTAMANANDA, a senior monk of the Ramakrishna Order, is the head of Sri Ramakrishna Math, Chennai. He is also a trustee of the Ramakrishna Math, and a member of the Governing Body of the Ramakrishna Mission.

SWAMI BHAJANANANDA, a former editor of the *Prabuddha Bharata,* is a senior monk of the Ramakrishna Order. He is an Assistant Secretary of the Ramakrishna Math and the Ramakrishna Mission, and lives at the Order's headquarters in Belur Math.

Dr. ANTHONY ALLINA, M.D., has a private family practice in Santa Barbara, California, USA, since 1978, with an emphasis on psychosomatic medicine. He has been a lecturer and instructor in Psychosomatic Medicine at the University of California (at Santa Barbara) and Antioch University.

PRAVRAJIKA VRAJAPRANA is a nun of the Vedanta Society of Southern California at Sarada Convent, Santa Barbara, USA. She is the author of *My Faithful Goodwin* (1992) and *A Portrait of Sister Christine* (1996). She has also edited *Living Wisdom: Vedanta in the West* (1994) and Swami Shraddhananda's *Seeing God Everywhere: A Practical Guide to Spiritual Living* (1996).

ELEANOR FOSTER, M.A., M.F.C.C., is a practising psychotherapist in Santa Cruz, California, USA. At present her work with the Religious Society of Friends is as chairperson of the committee to rewrite the Book of Faith and Practice for Pacific Yearly Meeting.

Dr. RALF DAMWERTH of Berlin, Germany, studied medicine in Great Britain and in the United States, and is now serving in the Jüdische Krankenhaus ('Jewish Hospital') in Berlin.

CARLA MARTINEZ is a published poet living on forty acres in the foothills of Santa Margarita, California, USA, where she walks the land with her dog Jenny, when it isn't too hot. Carla will soon be embarking on speaking engagements regarding healing.

SAM GRACI of British Columbia, Canada, has masters degrees in Adolescent Psychology and Chemistry. He began as an Adolescent Psychologist and realized that many behavioral imbalances have a dysfunctional nutritional pattern. Sam is presently a full-time specialist researching nutrition and the functions of the body. He is a well-known lecturer in both North America and Europe.

ELVIRA GRACI of British Columbia, Canada, is a nutritional researcher and author who researches natural foods as they appear in Nature, and the effect that these foods have on maintaining optimal good health in the human body. Involved in nutritional research with her husband Sam since 1980, she trains or demonstrates to people how to put Sam's research into practical application in the kitchen.

Dr. P. K. LALA, M.D., of Canada, received his medical training in Calcutta. His lifetime research (starting in the 1950s) has been on the mechanisms of Cancer development and its relationship to our immune system. Dr. Lala is currently professor at the Department of Anatomy and Cell Biology, Department of Oncology, and Department of Microbiology and Immunology at the University of Western Ontario. His research has led to a new mode of

Cancer Immunotherapy, which turns on certain killer cells of our immune system to destroy cancer cells.

Dr. M. LONNIE WU first trained as an R.N. in the U.S. and later became a Doctor of Oriental Medicine. On the faculty of the Santa Barbara College of Oriental Medicine, she is in practice with her son, Anthony. Dr. Wu was the first acupuncturist to serve on staff in a California hospital.

H. R. NAGENDRA, Ph.D., is director of Vivekananda Kendra Yoga Research Foundation, Bangalore. He is the author of 15 books on yoga and 16 research papers. He has presented 40 papers in leading yoga conferences.

CHRIS LOVATO is a student of Vedanta. She lives in Vancouver, Canada, where she is faculty member at the University of British Columbia. Chris has a Ph.D. in psychology and conducts research in health promotion and disease prevention.

Dr. H. SUDARSHAN, M.B.B.S., is founder of the Vivekananda Girijana Kalyana Kendra (VGKK), an integrated tribal development project at B.R. Hills in Karnataka. For his pioneering work, he has received several national and international awards, including the Right Livelihood Award (Alternate Nobel Prize) in 1994.

NANCY BROOKS of California, USA, graduated from Ventura College School of Nursing in 1973, and thereafter worked as a school nurse, managed a medical office, worked in home healthcare, hospital nursing, as a ship's nurse on a Caribbean cruise ship, then returned to home nursing. Holistic health has broadened the options available to her for teaching self-care and self-healing in home care and she continues to learn from every patient she works with.

RYOSUKE URYU of Japan is acupuncturist and doctor of Comfortable Medicine.

Dr. NARAS BHAT, M.D., F.A.C.P., of California, USA, is a professor of behavioral medicine at Rosebridge College of Integrative Psychology. He is also the founder and director of the Cybernetic Institute for Reversal of Heart Disease, located at Concord, California. Dr. Bhat is the author of *How to Reverse and Prevent Heart Disease and Cancer* and has produced two popular videos: *Uprooting Anger* and *Meditation Prescription*.

SWAMI TYAGANANDA, a monk of the Ramakrishna Order, has edited this volume. His essay appeared originally as an editorial in the *Vedanta Kesari*.